"Some of us church leaders believe to the core of our beings that the church is the only God-anointed agency in society that stewards the transforming message of the love of Christ ... into a whole new way of living and loving and serving, and can thereby transform society. ... We believe this to our depths. We'd take bullets for it."

—Bill Hybels, *Courageous Leadership*

Praise for

A PRACTICAL THEOLOGY
of ASSESSMENT

Seminaries have been good at teaching biblical content and skill development but we have often failed to take into account the natural talents our students bring with them. Without this knowledge often their future career decisions sadly take unnecessary wrong turns. This book is a great corrective illustration of how natural talents and ministry effectiveness can work together for the furtherance of God's kingdom.

—Norm Thiesen, PhD, Professor of Counseling

The material in this book provides some of my best "go to" resources when a student comes into my office wrestling with his or her calling in life. I use the talent assessment with all of my leadership students at the seminary. Truly a life changing blessing in my student's lives.

—George Hillman, MDiv, PhD, Department Chair
and Associate Professor, Educational Ministries and
Leadership, Dallas Theological Seminary

The combination of an assessment master craftsman, Bradley, and a discerning denomination executive, Wiggins, with the foresight for application has produced this valuable book. Both authors help our understanding of assessing God's design in peoples' lives and matching them to careers and ministry that will maximize their strengths. It is an invaluable resource for anyone who is in a position of coaching people toward their life callings. I have used these principles for over twenty-five years in the recruitment and placement of career missionaries.

—Jim Hamilton new staff recruiter, Interact Ministries,
Director of Engage Summer Ministry

The IDAK testing instrument is a major tool used in the Introduction to Ministry class I teach for undergraduate theology students. After using the information gleaned from the IDAK results, each student writes a lengthy paper about themselves. It is rewarding as a teacher to frequently read students comments stating that they now feel they can relax and be the person whom God gifted them to be and minister accordingly.

—Barry Tryon, DMin, Professor of Church Ministries
School of Religion, Southern Adventist University

This book will be a guide for you to clearly differentiate between your areas of talents and less-giftedness. Everyone is different. There is no right or wrong personal strengths and talent profile. The only wrong answer is to not know your strength and weaknesses, so as to manage your life and work for the best outcomes, the greatest joy. This is true whether you are in a marketplace or ministry job. We are strengthened by our strengths and weakened, burned out, by operating in areas of weakness. This book will give a practical basis, with a biblical foundation, to know thyself.

—Nelson Malwitz, Founder, Finishers Project/MissionNext

An excellent tool that has been crafted by careful theological reflection, sound application of social science research, and rigorous testing with many thousands of applications with congregational and church leaders. This model has proven to be a powerful tool for guiding and affirming the placement of individuals for Christian service. It is on the top of my list for a method that works for career placement in ministry.

—Rob Wiggins, PhD, Vice President for Academic Affairs and
Dean of the Faculty, Western Seminary

I have been using IDAK's natural talent assessments for over twenty years with seminary students, pastor candidates, and with pastors needing re-direction. The process helped me to encourage pastors and other ministry leaders to be energized by ministry and to create healthy expectations of ministry and life.

—Dr. Gary Floyd, Church Planting Catalyst,
Southern Baptist NW Convention

As a practicing therapist, I think this book is a must-read for denominational leaders who are interested in more effective church planting, and, frankly, for any believer who is confused regarding God's plan for their lives. I also believe that, without question, this resource should find a prominent place in every seminary library and in most ministry class curricula.

This book strips away the debilitating shame and negative self-characterizations that can result when we don't know more precisely the talents God has given us and how they can be used for the kingdom.

The authors buttress their arguments with a sound biblical theology that clarifies the concept of work in the believer's life and with a much needed distinction between natural talents and spiritual gifts.

—Gary H. Lovejoy, PhD, Founder, Valley View Counseling Services LLC

In applying these new IDAK insights, I have experienced reduced stress, increased joy, greater focus, increased productivity, and direction for lifelong learning.

—Jeff Norris, District Superintendent,
Western Pennsylvania District of the C&MA

When it was suggested that I go through the IDAK process, I was rather skeptical. As a result of the assessment process, the ministry choice I have made matches who I am and what I do best better than any other ministry I've been involved in.

—Chuck Kelley, President, Bridge Builders International

As a pastor's wife for over 40 years I have also served as president of pastor's wives association, and worked as an office manager and director of church music. I have used the IDAK talent assessment for over 30 years with countless numbers of women in ministry, including pastors wives and lay people. I have found that when a person knows what their God-given natural talents are it brings freedom to minister and joy in service.

—Carolyn Hagenbaugh, Corvallis, Oregon

A PRACTICAL THEOLOGY *of* ASSESSMENT

Discoveries from 25 Years of Assessing Ministry Candidates

Dr. Don Wiggins

Dr. John Bradley

A Practical Theology for Candidate Assessment: Discoveries from 25 Years of Assessing Ministry Candidates

ISBN: 978-0-9892622-5-5

We dedicate this book to four saints—
Kathy Taubeneck, Mary Johnson, Cindy Ludeman,
and Carolyn Hagenbaugh—who have worked tirelessly for
twenty-five years overseeing the administration of projects,
training notebooks, scheduling of training sessions, keeping
records, and so much more. Thank you for the faithful
encouragement and joy you have added to all this labor.

CONTENTS

Part V Adjustments and Improvements

ACKNOWLEDGMENTS

To give the impression that this large-scale, quarter-century work was completed by two individuals would be a gross error. Many people contributed through their letters, e-mails, and phone calls; some provided suggestions for improvement. Countless others volunteered their time to serve as practicum candidates during training, to assist as role-play coaches or actors, and to provide backup counseling and instruction. We express a special thanks to all the C&MA national leaders who affirmed and provided funding. Our appreciation goes to Dan Wetzel, vice president of Church Ministries, and Andy Kerr, assistant vice president, who provided the finances for this publication. We heartily thank Brian Smith for his tireless editing and most diplomatic prompting when we needed it. Also, a special thank you goes to Jackie Kludt and her very creative team for design, final editing and page layout. A special thank you goes to district leaders Jeff Norris and Jon Rich, who have given their time to further refine the training curriculum and provide coaching. Rosilio Roman, assistant vice president for multicultural church districts provided an incredible contribution for better understanding the needs of multicultural churches, both first- and second-generation pastors. Also, thanks to counselors Sarah McAfee, Tom Board, Tom Lyman, and Ron Sorensen for their assistance in coaching trainees. Dr. Gary Lovejoy and Dr. Greg Knopf were instrumental in helping demystify depression in ministry leaders. Jay Carty, during his advanced stages of illness, provided much editorial coaching and sage advice. We also want to acknowledge the repeated assistance provided by

Alliance Theological Seminary, Crown College, and Toccoa Falls College, who hosted our training events and provided practicum candidates from their student body. We both are humbled by all of your assistance and that of others too numerous to mention. A deep thank you.

FOREWORD

As vice president for Church Ministries with the Christian and Missionary Alliance, I have led the application of the IDAK interview and MAX Report assessment since 2007. During this time I have attended multiple training events and coached many of our field district superintendents in the application of this process. I am delighted to promote this celebration of twenty-five years of growth in the assessment of our future leaders. We have come a long way, and yet as this book states, we still have key hurdles ahead.

The IDAK assessment has proved to be an invaluable tool for screening new pastor candidates and for counseling Christian workers regarding their call to full-time ministry. I initially sought to be certified to use the tool when I was serving as a district superintendent. At the time I wanted some means to identify potential church planters and church-planting teams. And, the IDAK assessment quickly proved to have value in many other circumstances. Before long it became a standard means to assist pastors in times of transition and pastoral change. It was also valuable as a tool to help elders and other church leaders understand the dynamics of their relationships with each other and the pastoral team.

John Calvin began the *Institutes* by observing that no one can truly understand God without also understanding himself or herself. IDAK has proven to be a reliable and tested means for men and women who desire to serve God well by increasing their self-understanding, and so to grow in both competency and effectiveness in ministry.

I heartily encourage you to read this book with an open mind. It provides much of the wisdom we've learned from experience, which can benefit all who educate, recruit, and select future ministry leaders.

Dan Wetzel, Vice President of Church Ministries
The Christian and Missionary Alliance

INTRODUCTION

Building on a Beginning

Although almost every ministry organization has its own cultural paradigm regarding the assessment of leadership attributes, the turnover rate of management according to *Reference USA* is 50 percent every two years. It is no surprise then that a typical organization's method of assessment is endlessly in process, much like a train on a circular track returning to the starting point every few years.

The Christian and Missionary Alliance has survived this circular syndrome by affirming one core assessment theology and process for more than twenty-five years. *And beyond mere survival, we have effectively improved pastor placements and significantly increased the success of church plants.* In so doing, we have gained much experiential knowledge about effective screening and placement, as well as resolution of job performance conflicts. We have also learned, most importantly, how to realistically and optimally assess and guide young leaders in higher education aspiring to be future pastors. Now you can learn from our experience.

The pages in this book tell the story of how the two of us, with little initially in common, forged a twenty-five-year working relationship to develop a practical theology for pastor candidate assessment. Our story is not of introducing a well-developed plan, but of a process of trial and error that worked and gained the support of district officers. This field support nurtured ministry continuity even when changes in national senior leadership may have been inclined to consider other paradigms and systems.

Years of discovery preceded this book. Learning how to identify and put into words the elements of personhood. Developing assessment tools that help men and women discern their divinely designed makeup. And then refining their use in practice. Drawing from more than fifty combined years of experience, we share with you, the reader, what we've discovered and the story of how it was implemented throughout a major evangelical denomination, The Christian and Missionary Alliance (the C&MA, or the Alliance).

Although the majority of our assessment history has been with male students seeking to be senior pastors and experienced senior pastors applying for new church opportunities, the doctrine of natural talents and temperament traits has no gender preference—God has provided for both men and women all of the traits discussed in this book.

What you will find is an honest account of the ups and downs over twenty-five years. What worked and what didn't. Surprises along the way. And enduring principles that emerged.

We offer our findings, from both our successes and our failures, to several kinds of individuals: to those who guide and place ministry applicants; to those who educate future leaders; to those who seek to discover and maximize their God-given aptitudes and personality traits in ministry service; both to those preparing for ministry and to those already established in a ministry career; and to those in midlife who are seeking direction into another ministry venue.

We invite you to dream with us. Imagine the benefits in your sphere of influence when the theology and practice of Bible-based personal assessment is better understood and more widely implemented. We trust you will benefit from our experience as you help others seek their ideal roles in God's kingdom service, and as you do the same for yourself.

PART I

What We Thought Needed to Be Fixed

Chapter 1

Assessment Mythology

"For the LORD sees not as man sees: man looks on the outward appearance, but the LORD looks on the heart."
(1 Samuel 16:7, ESV)

I'm not against being all that we can be. I'm against the arrogance that tries to be something we're not.
—*Richard A. Swenson, MD,* Restoring Margin to Overloaded Lives

"We throw it on the wall and see what sticks."

He said it, but I (Don) couldn't believe my ears!

It was in the fall of 1990 in Chicago at a meeting with church-planting leaders from about twenty evangelical denominations. I was brand new to denominational leadership, after seventeen years of experience as a pastor and teacher. My task as a church health staff member in Church Ministries was to come alongside Fred King, the dynamic church-planting leader for The Christian and Missionary Alliance (C&MA), to strengthen new and existing churches through coaching and assessment.

This was my first taste of what was happening on the national scene, and I was in disbelief.

The eighties had been heady times for U.S. denomination-sponsored church planting. Due in part to the church-growth movement, many groups had reprioritized their national resources to focus on reaching spiritually lost people and altogether planting thousands of new churches within the U.S. Independent megachurches were a relatively new phenomenon. The strongest momentum for evangelism through church planting was found among evangelical denominations. That alone surprised me.

The Chicago gathering of church-planting directors was a venue for sharing ideas and resources and praying together for a harvest. Each leader was given time to present denominational goals, strategies, and how church planters were selected and deployed.

In answer to this last question—how to choose planters—one leader said, "We throw it on the wall and see what sticks." He went on to say that their success rate was only 25 percent, meaning that 75 percent of their church-planting projects failed. Not much was sticking! Other leaders nodded in agreement and obvious concern. That was the real shock: No one knew what to do.

Identifying Our True Problem

The frank assessment of what was happening struck a deep chord in me. My denomination did a little better, with a projected survival rate of 50 percent following a major thrust to plant one hundred new churches, all launched on Easter Sunday 1987. A thousand more new churches were envisioned from 1989 to 1994. However, the mounting number of casualties and lost resources brought out the skeptics. Was church planting truly worth it?

Even more appalling than the waste of dollars was the extensive damage to men and women who took big risks to attempt church plants but lived now with broken dreams and defeat. Surely Jesus did not have such failure in mind when He promised Peter and the disciples, "I will build my church, and the gates of Hades will not overcome it" (Matthew 16:18).

There has to be a better way to do church planting, I thought.

But what was it? The center of the problem seemed to be in the selection and training of the planter. What eluded me was how to know who should be recruited. What was it that set apart those

> **Even more appalling than the waste of dollars was the extensive damage to men and women**

intrepid church planters who succeeded from those who did not? I knew from close-up contact that church planting was hard work, calling for something out of the ordinary from the pioneer leader.

Though I had not led a church plant, as a pastor in Atlanta I had started a Bible study in a neighboring community that developed later into church plant. And in my pastorate in the Chicago suburbs, our church partnered with a nearby plant by commissioning a few families, prayer backing, personal support, and coaching.

Those experiences had given me no idea, really, of what to look for in the ideal church planter. Was it primarily a willing heart to volunteer for a tough assignment? Was it extraordinary zeal and passion? Was it an indefinable divine gift? Or should we be satisfied merely with whatever would stick on the wall?

So, on the way back to Colorado, I committed to finding out everything I could about the qualities that identified planters who were likely to thrive.

My colleague and friend, Fred King, a very successful church planter himself, had raised the bar by 1990. With his task force he drew up a detailed set of criteria for the best church planter candidates, related to calling, godly character, spiritual disciplines, certain personality traits, and spousal agreement. The description even contained a few specific initiatives Fred and others had found to be successful—like becoming a local police chaplain. I found the list daunting enough that I wondered who but a few commando types could qualify!

And we had a second problem. Not only were the criteria many, we also lacked definitions for what we wanted. For example, being "a people person" or "self-disciplined" were surprisingly vague terms. They were defined differently in the eye of each individual beholder, usually according to personal preference. Even fuzzier was the commonly used term "a really sharp couple"—everyone was looking for them! But what did that mean? No one could say for sure.

So, with our list of qualities as yet unclear, it's no wonder that many church-planting leaders were not sure how to identify the most promising people. Too much reliance was placed on measures such as educational degrees or training-seminar certificates. And we were too easily talked into (or in some cases, talked ourselves into) lifting up self-promoting persons who talked a good game but, as it turned out, did not often have what it took to successfully plant a church.

We were perfect evidence of the astutely simple truth of Peter Drucker's statement: "Most people think they know what they are good at. They are usually wrong. More often, people know what they are not good at—and even then more people are wrong than right. And yet, a person can perform only from strength. One cannot build performance on weaknesses, let alone on something one cannot do at all."[1] God was good in spite of our foibles, to be sure. Scores of church-planting candidates with strong qualifications were identified and placed. They led thousands to faith in Jesus Christ, making true disciples in dozens of new churches across North America in the 1980s. But it was obvious to all that there were far too many false starts and human casualties along the way to be acceptable. We needed to do much better at choosing those truly qualified for start-up church planting.

Searching for Answers

How? I wondered. Was there anyone out there who could help us?

My prayers for answers led me into a conversation a few months later with one of our district superintendents—Loren Calkins—who had served in Texas and pastored in Oregon. He told me about an organization named IDAK—and its president, John Bradley—that had helped him figure out his aptitude strengths as they related to ministry.

I'd never heard of IDAK, but after reading the materials Loren sent to me (no website back then!), I was intrigued by John Bradley's claim that their tools could match up job descriptions (including ministry roles) with well-defined aptitude strengths. The name IDAK represents a person's unique identity: ID = identity plus AK = the Hebrew equivalent of uniqueness. As a veteran of umpteen seminars and personality tests, I was more than a little skeptical. IDAK was probably another sort of overly simple "test" that pigeon-holed everyone in one quadrant or another and labeled them for life, or so I thought.

But I was desperate enough to follow up on the lead. So I contacted IDAK, warily, to be sure. Before long, John Bradley and I met over breakfast when he came to visit one of his clients, Denver Seminary. My specific question to him was how to identify startup church planters. Could he help us find more? What he explained that morning was not at all what I expected or had ever heard before. He listened to my litany of needed qualifications and traits. And then he said, "Don, this is so complicated, you will never find enough people to plant one thousand more churches. From my experience and research, there is *one* bottom-line trait that separates the possible church planters from all the rest of your ministry candidates. Do you think John would tell me that *one* trait? He hinted but did not give me much. Perhaps he knew he had me on the hook. If so, he was right. Before long, I invited John for a follow-up meeting with Fred, John Ng, another colleague, and me at our Colorado Springs offices.

> *From my experience and research, there is* one *bottom-line trait that separates the possible church planters from all the rest of your ministry candidates.*

The Aha Moment

In that meeting in late 1990, we showed John our written list of new-start qualifications. John examined it for a few minutes and then demonstrated his ability to diagnose job descriptions and determine the key one or two talents that were essential for successful job performance. He looked us straight in the eyes and told us that we had way too many criteria to ever find the number of new-start church planters we wanted.

There was just *one* indispensable trait, and he could help us identify people with it. IDAK's paradigm, its theological base, the inventory tools to be used—all of that was interesting stuff—but the three of us wanted to know the *one* trait!

Finally, John disclosed the secret: "The bottom line for church planting, bar none, is what we call the Initiating/Developing talent. Assuming that the person has a strong marriage and is spiritually mature, this is the talent that makes all the difference."

"What exactly is Initiating/Developing?" we asked.

"It's more commonly referred to as the *entrepreneur* talent," he explained. "It includes the ability to cast a compelling vision, recruit others to join to accomplish that vision, and then hold their feet to the fire to get it done. It's not merely conceiving a vision or promoting it to others, but gathering and galvanizing a group that will join together and accomplish it."

That was it? I confess to initial disappointment. How could that talent be the make-or-break factor?

We let it sink in for a few minutes as John explained what this aptitude looks like in operation. Of course, John was not saying that all the other factors on our list didn't matter. He was showing us the single most important thing to look for.

I think he saw doubt on our faces, so he explained it another way: "If you have three candidates with equally strong character, calling, pulpit communication, and marriages, what will make one most likely to succeed in planting a new church?" The "startup" talent would be the difference. And nothing else would make up for its absence.

"So, John, let's suppose this is true. How do you know if someone has the 'church start' talent? How can you tell?"

The *how* question was just as important to me as the *what* question. If there was one bottom-line talent, we'd better be able to find out if a candidate has it!

"Well," John said, "a person with this talent will have a track record of startups in their adult experience, even starting with high school. They will have been a starter in a variety of ways— like starting a business, a team, or an organization, or even a new ministry from the ground up in a church. The key is that they have proven ability to gather other people around them and make it happen. It won't have happened once. It will have happened successfully multiple times. When you find that track record, you are identifying the Initiating/Developing talent."

Now it was making sense to me. The ability to be that catalyst might indeed be our bottom line. And if we could learn to identify it, that would the clincher. That appealed to me. Going on hunches, inadequate interviews, and résumé claims just wasn't good enough. A whole new level of certainty finally seemed attainable. I knew it definitely was worth pursuing.

> *A person with this talent will have a track record of startups in their adult experience, even starting with high school.*

That was the *aha* moment for me. It was the first step that pointed the C&MA onto a twenty-five-year path filled with stories of empowered people planting churches across the U.S. I can look back on that initial insight now with great joy and gratitude.

With so much at stake, it seemed very important that some of us would go through an IDAK professional assessment. Whether or not we checked out as church planters, the experience alone would be helpful to validate John's claims. Dr. John Ng and I volunteered to be the guinea pigs. For both of us, the assessment was very enlightening.

On my part, as a forty-year-old, I did not discover new areas of aptitude. I knew most of my strengths intuitively. So when the assessor gave me the results, I nodded my head on almost every point. What was insightful was the specific name of a talent and its behavioral pattern. "So that's what you call it!" was my reaction. It was like flipping on the light switch in a room previously lit by a candle.

For example, seminar presentation settings with lots of give and take were much more comfortable for me than settings that called for delivering a straight lecture. I found it easy to be up in front of all sizes of groups, so why the difference? My assessor shared that there is a specific up-front talent called Giving Presentations with Audience Interaction. The person motivated by this talent seeks to communicate with groups in an interactive manner—making use of dialogue and questions and answers, and observing body language and facial expressions. I preferred this two-way speaking venue and found it energizing. Based on a long list of specific examples, my assessor offered his opinion that Giving Presentations was indeed a strong innate aptitude for me.

Naming the talent validated its presence. It also helped clarify why I was drawn to want to communicate in front of others but was not energized to be seeking the pulpit every week (which is a distinct talent, I learned). I saw that my talent was something more than a learned skill or a communication technique. It was innate, built-in part of my hardwiring. That's why, even when I utilized it frequently and intensely, the experience was energizing and not draining.

My coworker, Dr. John Ng, had a similarly rich experience of putting terms to his specific traits. We were now ready to commit to move ahead.

Pilot Project

The next step was to see if our personal experiences could be duplicated among district leaders. In late 1991, we invited six district leaders to participate in a pilot project in assessment training. They themselves were assessed and given basic training in the IDAK paradigm of natural talents. Even the most veteran members of the pilot group agreed that it was powerful, if not revolutionary. For example, one district leader in his sixties remarked that this approach to assessment and placement would entirely change his job! Instead of simply moving pastors from one assignment to another, he could now begin to empower each of them with a knowledge of personal aptitude strengths and match them with the right church.

Even the most veteran members of the pilot group agreed that it was powerful, if not revolutionary.

We not only learned the difference between God-given talents and spiritual gifts, but how to separate out temperament or personality traits. In addition, we learned how to do the assessment ourselves in our own offices as well as over the lunch table, without having to go back to John or one of his colleagues. John was teaching us to conduct the very same assessment that he had developed beginning in 1980.

With this pilot received well, we set out to systematically train all the twenty-two geographical district superintendents, and we provided basic-level training to those working in cultures where English was a second language. If we could train all these leaders to successfully screen candidates, our church-planting assessment problems would go away.

At least that's what we hoped.

Chapter 2
Assessment Discovery

O Lord, you have searched me
*   and you know me. (Psalm 139:1)*

No organization can depend on genius; the supply is
always scarce.... The purpose of an organization is to
enable common men [and women] to do uncommon things.
—Peter Drucker, Management

We were on our way. We now were successfully applying a proven talent-screening method to church-planting candidates. The most important problem was solved.

Or was it? I (John) saw a deeper, more essential issue. In my experience of assessing individuals over the previous years, along with the combined experience of my IDAK colleagues in different cities and states, the Initiating/Developing talent has been found to be rare. Approximately 10-15 percent of the population has this innate talent. So even though we were screening for the talent among candidates who were coming to us, the talent is so uncommon that we needed to learn how to do more than passively wait for them to come; we needed to go out and find them. We needed a better recruitment process to find and gather talented church-planter candidates.

The need for this particular innate talent sets the bar high for qualification, but we've learned from hard experience the damage that can be done by lowering the standards. The sparseness of qualified candidates mandates casting a larger net to find those who are gifted for the job.

The Christian & Missionary Alliance in the United States has four college campuses and one seminary that provide the bulk of their pastor candidate pool. To select out those with the church-planter talent should be a priority. However, after visiting with each of the campus presidents and faculty, no lasting recruitment program has been established. Recruiting these up-and-coming entrepreneurs requires more than a potluck for interested candidates. Nor is it as simple as screening all students who apply for church ministry as a major. A young man with this talent is considerably different from the other 85 percent of males. He can be somewhat of a renegade, one who writes his own rules. Perhaps one who challenges portions of the student handbook. He might be found to live on the wild side, to break the rules, to pull pranks, to lead a protest, to confront issues with vigor, and so on. In short, the very students who qualify based on talent may be headed in the direction of starting their own company, starting their own ministry, pioneering a new mission project overseas, or some other adventurous endeavor. Most likely these individuals would not be encouraged by a professor to pursue the pastorate, as their student behavior might not be considered appropriate for a church leader.

> *A young man with this talent is considerably different from the other 85 percent of males.*

It is interesting that Bill Hybels was recruited as a college student by his professor to consider the pastorate as an alternate path from his plan for a career in business. Two other Initiator/Developers are Rick Warren and Dr. James Dobson—both of whom started their ministries from scratch and continued to innovate beyond the startup phase.

A second viable source for church planters is midcareer and early retirement Christians who have been successful in starting their own businesses. When introduced to the opportunity, many such individuals and couples respond positively to God's prompting to consider ministry service. Very little is being done to attract this tremendous pool of potential church-planter candidates.

In short, the real problem in discovering gifted church planters has not been the screening process, but the lack of a proactive recruitment, which would provide more qualified candidates to choose from. When those responsible for placement end up with too few qualified candidates, their temptation is to substitute other talent traits in the place of the Initiating/Developing trait—traits that are well suited to other roles and might appear to fit the church-planter job description, but end only in failure when matched with that task. This new insight about the scarcity of qualified church-planter candidates was a new hurdle we had not anticipated. Still to this day, finding qualified candidates is a challenge.

Bonus Discoveries

Though our original intent was only to fix the problems with identifying church-planter candidates, we found that the assessment process had a much wider range of applications.

For example, we soon realized that established pastors, regardless of their interest in church planting, could benefit from an aptitude assessment. For one thing, it could affirm to them what they thought were their strengths, and help them focus energy and time on those areas. For another, it could help them identify areas of ministry—non-strengths—where they needed staff or volunteers to come alongside them.

Several Alliance districts—at least five—devoted their annual pastors' retreat to hosting John and working through his assessment process. Wives were encouraged to participate as well, since many ministry couples share ministry as a team. These events included small group or individual follow-up by the superintendent or another trained individual. The reports coming back from superintendents indicated a widespread sense of empowerment among pastors.

One Pennsylvania pastor personally came to Don at the next national denominational conference excited to share that the discoveries he made had revolutionized his ministry—finally giving him confidence and freedom to focus on identified ministry strengths instead of seeking to excel in all areas. He also allowed himself to intentionally delegate areas of non-strength to his capable staff members. Everyone was much happier, he said—both his wife and his staff—with the new dynamics.

Another application was the assessment of incoming applicants and those in their early years of service, not just for church planting, but for any ministry role. The importance of a positive start cannot be overstated. Too many promising candidates drop out primarily because they have negative ministry experiences that knock them off their feet. One way to address that vulnerability is to develop self-awareness. Knowledge of one's aptitude strengths and non-strengths can be a lifesaver to young pastors. It steers them toward the areas where they can excel and be energized over a lifetime of ministry. And it defines the areas where they must learn to at least be adequate and accept limitations. Bill Hybels challenges all of us: "When I ask leaders who have disqualified themselves from ministry why they didn't make changes that would have made their life more sustainable, the most frequent answer is, 'I didn't have the guts. I couldn't muster the courage. ... I didn't want them thinking I wasn't a team player.'"[2]

One of the most difficult tasks for ministry supervisors is placing those workers who prove to be marginally productive in ministry. The easy "answer" is to shuffle them from small church to small church every few years. A more direct (and disastrous) approach is to wash them out of ministry altogether. I (Don) saw both these tendencies in my own fellowship and found them troubling. Too many of these well-meaning individuals end up wounded, disillusioned, and embittered. Such an outcome is unnecessary when in fact they could be helped and possibly redirected to a better-fitting leadership role.

We learned to apply the assessment process to those not doing well in local church ministry. Some couples were helped to overcome personal and marital issues or to address person-ality traits that hindered healthy ministry. In other cases, we redirected failing pastors toward successful ministry outside of local church leadership. I personally witnessed several strug-gling pastors make the transition into chaplaincy roles where they then thrived. Their sense of divine call had been affirmed, but in a different role and venue.

Finally, district leaders were perpetually perplexed about churches in decline that needed to turn around, sometimes through a drastic redevelopment process or a district-supported restart. District leaders tried various tools and strategies, but the evidence pointed again and again to and often-overlooked reality: To make a lasting turnaround, a church with chronically declining membership needed a pastoral leadership change. And that needed to happen first, before other new strategies were launched. But what kind of pastoral leader did it take?

We developed a "turnaround pastor" profile and related it to a short list of required innate talent strengths. For this pastoral role, we added another key talent—namely, Problem Solving—as essential for the job. The list of qualifications ended up very similar to the church-planting list. Upon reflection, that should be no surprise. Redeveloping and rebuilding a church is just as daunting a project as launching a new church, often even a greater challenge. Whereas a new church has no history or tradition, every existing church deals with its past. The turnaround pastor comes into that context and attempts to bring change. That requires breaking some bad patterns and setting healthy ones in place. No small task. It helped to view these churches' needs through the talent lens when recruiting new leaders for that specialized task.

These bonus discoveries helped propel the popularity of the assessment process. It was gratifying to reap the harvest of the deep biblical and theological preparatory work that John and his team had done since 1980.

PART II

Theological and Biblical Foundation

Chapter **3**

A Practical Theology of Assessment

So God created man in his own image, in the image of God he created him; male and female he created them.
(Genesis 1:27)

In the hearts of all who are skillful I have put skill.
(Exodus 31:6, NASB)

Wisdom's function in Scripture is to put godliness into working clothes; to name business and society as spheres in which we are...to look for God's training.
—*Derek Kidner,* Commentary on Proverbs

When I (John) first started assessing aptitudes in 1972, there were few if any theological publications available to guide my efforts. The idea of a list of God-given traits was unheard of.

My first introduction to aptitude assessment was the challenge of separating "innate skills" from "learned skills" during my employment with a Fort Worth, Texas, headhunting firm. Returning from Vietnam, I needed a job to support my discipleship training with The Navigators under the direction of Gordon

and Brenda Van Amburgh. I sought the assistance of an employment agency. The agency owner, Ike DuBose, liked my previous
headhunting experience before military service, so he offered me
a job. Providentially, his was no ordinary recruiting firm. Back
then we were in the middle of President Lyndon Johnson's push
for affirmative action, to hire minorities to meet a quota. Large
companies were scrambling to find qualified African Americans
(then referred to as blacks), who could do jobs which only whites
had held for fifty years. Our firm was contracted to identify candidates for positions where they had no outside sales experience.
And further, I was the only white in an all-black company. Just
how was I to determine if a high school science teacher could
sell pharmaceuticals for the big giants, Johnson and Johnson,
Eli Lilly, and Upjohn, or work successfully for IBM and Xerox?

Ike was an incredible recruiter. He would enter an elevator,
and if he encountered an African American wearing a suit, before
the elevator reached the top floor, Ike would have the person's
business card and would have closed him on a job paying four
times what he was currently making.

When the individuals came to our office, Ike would send
them to my desk to "test" their sales ability. Peeling the onion
of a person's skill set was a trial-and-error effort. First, I had to
force myself to not stereotype the candidate by his occupation,
such as high school science teacher, custodian, or department
store clerk. I recall handing a client a can of soup and saying,
"Sell this to me." If I thought he did a good job, I referred him
back to Ike, who then coached him to prepare for a job interview.
After the first twenty-five or so candidates, I began to develop
a routine of questions such as, Did you ever sell items to raise
money at school, start your own lemonade stand, sell anything
door to door, or the like? Looking back, I now recognize this
as the very beginning of the autobiographical interview, which
has become the highest level of talent assessment validation.
While I listened to the candidate's answers, I was looking for

some spark of animation or excitement, indicating enthusiasm for such promotional and extroverted activities. I had engaged in small-scale sales activities in my youth, and I instinctively knew that these were accurate predictors of success in the fields for which we were recruiting. I didn't realize it at the time, but I was beginning the process of discovering a natural talent by evaluating one's behavioral patterns. Eventually, the evaluation process began to provide results. We then used this very same sales history as a selling point to promote the individuals to potential employers. I learned that one's past behavioral pattern provided much fertile ground for discovering one's innate talents—even more valuable than the usual listing of prior work experience. African Americans typically had no prior experience selling for Fortune 500 giants, but we used other related past activities as indicators of untapped talent.

Back then the idea of aptitude assessment as a qualifier for ministry leadership was frowned on, and in some circles considered sinful.

It was then that I sensed a prompting from God to make my life's work the assessment and counseling of individuals to discover their true callings. Back in the early seventies little had been written concerning a biblical approach to understanding our gifting. Most of the prevailing thought was that if God wanted you in ministry, He would tell you, just as He had told Moses, Isaiah, Samuel, Paul, and many others. Back then the idea of aptitude assessment as a qualifier for ministry leadership was frowned on, and in some circles considered sinful.

Assessment Grows Up

After two years I left my headhunting job in Texas to pursue a career counseling position at the University of California, Davis (my alma mater). The director of career planning, Russ Brusch, was intrigued about my quest to assess skills and talents. The prevailing national leader of career guidance thinking at that time was Richard Bolles, a former Episcopalian priest who had written the best-seller, *What Color Is Your Parachute?* While a priest, Bolles had received a grant to learn what secular professionals were doing in terms of career planning. Among several practitioners he drew from, he found two particularly valuable—John Crystal, the grandfather of all assessment, and Bernard Haldane, a former intelligence analyst from World War II. He built on their work in developing his eclectic book to help individuals discover their wiring.

Parachute, along with books by several other authors—such as Strong and Campbell, John Holland, Sidney Fine, Howard Figler, and Anthony Medley—began to help me explore the breadth of aptitude assessment. I was given permission to research aptitude assessment systems and to experiment with them to find something that could help our students. Yet my yearning was to know what God's Word had to say about this important topic, rather than merely to follow secular practitioners and testing systems. Finding little such information, and no biblically based assessment instrument, I began to explore seminaries who would allow me to pursue a master's degree on the topic of discovering what God's Word says about human aptitudes and calling for marketplace and ministry occupations.

Western Seminary in Portland, Oregon, agreed to allow my pursuit in the context of a Master of Divinity program. During my first year, I quickly identified a professor, Dr. Grant Howard, who chaired the department of practical theology. He was quite interested in my special focus on assessing natural talents and agreed to assist me. We met two hours a week for six months to discuss (and debate) the topic, blending his leadership paradigms with my journey into aptitude assessment. While a student at seminary I had secured a part-time position as director of career planning at a nearby campus, Warner Pacific College, where I taught a career-planning class. By this time I had developed a computerized scored version of what now is referred to as the Talent Discovery Guide, which I used with my students.

Grant and I met weekly in the faculty conference room. He would put his feet up on the boardroom table, lean back in the chair, and say, "What do you have for me today, young man?" It was up to me to come with two hours of subject matter for him to evaluate and critique. He would often ask, "Where do you find that in the Bible?" Or, "Where did you get that?" These meetings culminated in a one-week Leadership Lab seminar, which we taught to ten ministry leaders whom Grant selected from Western alumni. The seminar, which continued for the next five years, became the foundation material for developing my assessment process and for the foundation of IDAK Group, which Grant helped me and several others launch.

Concurrent with my sessions with Grant, I recall a burning-bush/Damascus-road type of event while sitting in Dr. Carl Laney's Old Testament Pentateuch survey class. We were studying Exodus, the building of the Tabernacle, chapter 25 and following. In 36:1-5 God instructed Moses that He had prepared two individuals to perform the tasks for building the Tabernacle. In later chapters we learn that these men were actually to serve as overseers of the project. In 31:6 the clouds parted for me. I read, "In the hearts of all who are skillful, I have given skill" (NASB). That was the key Scripture I was looking for—God declaring that He had created us with innate ability to do certain tasks. I realized right then that my quest was to identify the skills (talents) that God has given each person and then to develop a process to assess those talents.

As I further studied this passage, I found that the Hebrew word for "skill," *chokmah*, is also translated "wisdom." *How could that be?* I thought. How could skill be synonymous with wisdom? I did a quick word study and found that *chokmah* is used 146 times in the Old Testament, most often translated "wisdom," rather than "skill." The key Bible references were found in Proverbs 2, where a father advises his son to pursue wisdom. It is the most important thing in this world to seek—more precious than silver, gold, and jewels. I thought, *How can this be—wisdom more important than one's income and material acquisitions?*

What I found after further study became the core foundation for the practical theology that drove most everything I did from that day forward. I learned that to pursue wisdom meant the quest to find one's *chokmah,* one's God-given skill, and that pursuit was the most valuable. Finding one's innate skill would become the defining moment for one's vocational direction. If one were to follow that direction of further polishing and applying that skill, then it would reward him or her far more than silver, gold, and jewels ever could.

> *I learned that to pursue wisdom meant the quest to find one's chokmah, one's God-given skill.*

So there it was. The quest to discover one's innate God-given skills and then to apply those skills to an occupational goal was a worthy pursuit. The study of the wisdom (innate know-how) passages dominated my professional study for the next ten years. I began to experiment with all manner of tests and exercises to find skills that were innate, and then methods to discover them. I was fortunate to receive a $500,000 research grant to assist me in that study to develop a computer-scored career-guidance instrument—the IDAK Career Match—which would assist an individual in the pursuit of his and her *chokmah.* This grant allowed me to expand my research to include the help of other professionals, looking for any published book, article, or more importantly, vocational tests that identified innate traits. I also was able to contract the services of Dr. Robert

Larzelere at Rosemead Graduate School of Psychology to provide the valuable psychometrics so necessary for determining test validity and reliability. He in turn recruited a grad student, Arv Leighton, who shaped his doctoral dissertation around the evaluation of IDAK's Career Match in terms of validity and reliability. This independent audit of our instrument provided us with an unbiased verification of the instrument's accuracy in testing for natural talents.

Through these resources and procedures, a list of fifty-four innate talents emerged. The list was then validated by matching it to over 60,000 career options, ensuring that our team had not omitted any talents that 60,000 career options required. The fifty-four talents have stood the test of the next thirty-two years of practical application through six hundred counselors, educators, and consultants who have been trained to use the Career Match system (approximately 150 of these within the C&MA district offices). Those counselors and educators have tested well over 30,000 individuals throughout the U.S. and Canada.

Through these resources and procedures, a list of fifty-four innate talents emerged.

Scriptural Basics

As my study of God's Word continued, I found additional passages that clarified and expanded my theology of God's design in creating men and women.

From Genesis 1:26-27 we learn that we are created beings endowed with the likeness of God. This means that we did not evolve from genetic material, but that each of us has value and is given divine worth.

In Exodus 31:1-6, we learn that God gives skill and wisdom to apply to specific tasks. He named men previously recognized as craftsmen to build the temple with skill and knowledge given by the Spirit. According to commentators Karl Keil and Friedrich Delitzsch, "This did not preclude either natural capacity or acquired skill, but rather *presupposed* them" (emphasis added). And in the words of Robert Jamieson, A.R. Fausset and David Brown's commentary, "It is likely that He had given to the son of Uri that *strong natural aptitude* and those opportunities of gaining mechanical skill [in Egypt].... His natural and acquired gifts appeared to be *enlarged* and *invigorated* for the important work" (emphasis added).

The precision of this passage should not be overlooked. The instructions that God gave to Moses for the construction of the Tabernacle, were to be performed by men and women whom God had gifted. Not only did each craftsperson have innate talent, but each also had years of experience developing that talent to be worthy of this new special assignment. We see here that talent is most valuable and effective when polished through years of experience and application.

In Psalm 139:13-16 we learn that we are intricately woven in our mother's wombs. Every detail of our individual physical and spiritual makeup is known and appointed by God. No one is a number in a sea of humanity. I would add here that the very nature of our aptitudes was assigned to us at God's discretion, so that there was an appropriate distribution of traits to fulfill the multitudes of roles in the world.

From Ephesians 2:10 we see that we are created for good works. This means that the creative act of inventing each of us was for positive impact on the world, for eternity.

In Proverbs 22:29 we observe that to be a highly skilled worker is favorable to God. For these men and women are rewarded with the privilege of standing before kings. Thus God blesses the desire to master one's craft, as long as we give the glory to Him who gave us the gift.

In Isaiah 45 we read that God is the Potter and we the clay. Just to be sure the Old Testament reader got the point, Isaiah went on to say, *Who are we to argue?* (my paraphrase). Far too often in my counseling office I have witnessed men and women trying to reconstruct their aptitude profile to fulfill their own agendas. In essence they are saying, "I am not happy with the design God gave me. I need to add a few traits that God left out."

Along the way I felt a nagging frustration. Why were so many men and women who sought out seminary education doing poorly, in some cases failing in their work? Shouldn't these, more than those pursuing secular work, be able to discern God's *chokmah* in them? Further, I was troubled by several who dropped out of seminary, whom I felt had the desirable traits needed to pastor. My informal survey told me that these drop-outs failed to see the relevance of classroom instruction to the job. I recall one young pastor who came to me by reference of his father. I learned that the father had been a seminary student, dropped out, and started a successful real estate agency. The father confided in me that perhaps his son could fulfill the ministry vision that he had not been able to complete. After so many years the sting of dropping out was still fresh within this father.

> *Why were so many men and women who sought out seminary education doing poorly?*

As I began to serve these individuals as clients, I found that they had formed their own images of what they felt was the most honorable leadership role, and then sought to use academic education and field experience to fill in what God had chosen to leave out. Looking back, I feel this is one of the most critical issues that defines the four soils (Luke 8:4-15). The rocky soil and the thorn-infested soil represent individuals who are not willing to bend the knee to the *chokmah* that God has put in them. They are arguing with the Potter, saying, I know better!

This is a sad commentary on the preparation of our men and women seeking to serve the King. Part of the assessment task often involves cutting through that smoke screen to discover the true core of a person.

I then found portions of Scripture that focused on the selection of able and skilled men and women, including the building of the temple (2 Chronicles 2:7-8,13-14). King Saul was selected for obvious outward traits and was contrasted with David and his inward "heart" (1 Samuel 16:7). That portion of Scripture became pivotal, as I wanted to be able to look into the heart, rather than be dazzled by the outward appearance of a person's potential (job title, academic degrees, and the like).

Spiritual Gifts and Natural Talents

Because my MDiv degree program placed a significant emphasis on the study of Greek, I was able to dig into the thorny issue of how spiritual gifts compared with the *chokmah* gifts (natural talents). My classes did not include any teaching regarding the *chokmah* gifts. However, knowing one's spiritual gifts was taught as essential to identifying and qualifying for ministry service. After many sessions with Grant Howard, we were able to carve out a biblically based explanation concerning the two categories of aptitudes, which we taught in our seminars. We explained that talents are applicable in both sacred and secular work (such as that of the tabernacle craftsmen), and that one's natural talents are among the best indicators of the type of work for which is one is best suited. Spiritual gifts, on the other hand, were a distinct kind of empowerment to do supernatural tasks, such as Moses' miracles, the prophets' predictions of the future, and the apostles' and Paul's miraculous healings and speaking in tongues.

I observed a great real-life illustration of the contrast between spiritual gifts and natural talents when Dr. Billy Graham visited Portland, Oregon, for a crusade. I encouraged my family to get involved. My wife and I volunteered for the peer counseling of individuals who came forward. We attended training meetings for several weeks and were impressed and excited. Finally the night came and Dr. Graham spoke. His advanced age at the time caused him to hesitate and lose his train of thought.

At the end, my junior high son turned to me and said, "Dad, was that it? It wasn't that great, was it?"

I thought for a moment and then pointed to the masses that were coming forward to the stadium floor. Thousands were quietly moving forward.

I said, "Dave, look there. That is the real test." We were observing something supernatural. No feat of clever speech by a naturally talented preacher motivated those individuals to step forward. God had done a supernatural miracle by way of a spiritual gift.

Spiritual gifts are used by the Holy Spirit sporadically, whereas we depend on our natural talents every day, and so talents are better pointers toward one's best career choices. We worked hard for twenty years to clarify these distinctions throughout the C&MA, hoping and expecting that the dominant appeal of spiritual gifts over natural talents would eventually fade. Little did I realize that the fascination with spiritual gifts would continue to the present day and continues to be a watershed issue for some of the Alliance district superintendents. This issue is such a potential distraction and entails such potential misunderstandings that Don and I have developed a more compatible explanation, which Don details later in this book.

Personality and Temperament Traits

Another discovery from the New Testament relates to the selection of ministry leaders who would lead the church. First there was Stephen and the other six deacons in Acts 6. These were to be men of good reputation, full of the Spirit and *wisdom*. A consensus from the community made the initial selection. Later in 1 Timothy 3 and Titus 1, Paul directed his two subordinates to select pastors (overseers) who demonstrated good character. None of the listed traits had anything to do with talent (*chokmah*) or spiritual gifts. The lists described one's personality or temperament traits. So, seeking to be obedient to the text, I acknowledged that temperament or personality traits needed to factor into the assessment process. Yet all Christians are encouraged to adopt these traits, implying that these traits can be learned, as opposed to talents, which are innate and can not be learned. Also, I noted that a central theme in Proverbs was to imitate certain behaviors of creatures—the ant in particular, which demonstrated self-discipline by being diligent with its time (Proverbs 6:6-8). So not only were a person's talents important to God, but also his or her adherence to certain behavioral patterns, defined as temperament traits. I found that these aptitudes could be measured by psychological testing for qualities such as Character, Self-Discipline, Hostility, Dominance, and others. Later in my continued study I found that psychologists generally agreed that temperament or personality traits are partially (about 30 percent) innate, and the rest (70 percent) are developed by positive and negative conditioning from parents, church, school, and society. Also, for Christians a large positive influence comes from the inner working of the Holy Spirit.

Many pieces were coming together to form a paradigm of one's attributes, separating out those traits that are uniquely from God versus a person's other traits. This clarifying paradigm came to be called the six suitcases (which we discuss in a later chapter). Assisted by my friend Jay Carty—a former client, one-time Los Angeles Laker, church-growth consultant, and speaker-evangelist—we coauthored a book and video discussion guide entitled *Discovering Your Natural Talents*. Jay, also a gifted writer, helped me to wordsmith many of the biblical principles I was using into a cohesive process that could be easily communicated to clients and seminar participants.

One additional observation is appropriate to include. There has been much written and spoken about the term *servant leader*. Jesus is often referred to as the ultimate Servant Leader, after whom we are to model our leadership style. However, when we look at His apostles, we find that their behavioral patterns in terms of leadership vary significantly based on their gifting. For example, contrast the aggressive church-planting style of Paul with the more mild style of John and the more impulsive style of Peter.

We propose the following understanding of the term *servant leader* as it applies to the manifestation of the natural talents and temperament traits of a leader. We use the agricultural and sheep-caretaking contexts of the New Testament era. A master gardener serves the plants in the garden by providing the right amount of water, nutrition, sun, or shade to help the plant grow to its fullest potential. But pruning and replanting are also part of the gardener's vigorously proactive role, taking charge of the garden and making decisions in the best interest of the garden members, the plants.

We see similar imagery in the picture of the caretaker of sheep. David fought lions and bears to protect his flock. He would lead them to green pastures and to quiet waters. Those who know sheep have stated that they can be rebellious and therefore sometimes need reprimand and punishment. All of these activities are intentional and proactive, not passive. The shepherd serves the sheep by ensuring that their needs are met and that they are safe and can grow to be healthy and strong.

These illustrations differ greatly from the "servant leader" sometimes depicted as serving at the beck and call of the served, subordinated to the assigned occupational level of his "followers." Biblically, we define a servant leader pastor as one who is vigilant, continuously looking out for his congregation, standing in the gap, providing biblical instruction, and meting out spiritual correction when needed. This is a robust, proactive leadership role, not that of a tired old padre whose ministry is limited to listening to his congregation's confessions and providing comfort and reassurance. This is an excellent example of the nuances that must be considered in the exercise of a pastor's gifting.

Cultural and Gender Observations

Because the majority of our pastoral assessment was focused on American or domestic church planters and then senior pastors in general, we did not gain much experience in assessing foreign national (cross-cultural) candidates or assessing women who aspired to church ministry roles. As of the writing of this book, I (John) am working with the Multi-Cultural Ministries leadership of The Christian and Missionary Alliance to determine a way to accurately assess God's talents in those cultures while honoring the cultural distinctions. We are very early in our discovery stages. The good news for us is that we have the favorable cooperation and availability of many pastors representing those cultures who will guide us in the journey of discovery.

Our assessment of women seeking to serve in ministry and more specifically in church ministry has been very limited. Don and I hold to the interpretation of 1 Timothy 3, which affirms men for the position of senior pastor (including church planter). This, however, would not preclude women from aspiring to other church leadership roles. Also, my independent experience apart from my work for the Alliance has shown repeatedly that women, like men, have been gifted with all the talents, including the Supervisory talents of Initiating/Developing, Planning, and Managing.

Conclusion

Looking twenty-five years ahead, the future of how talents of men and women are assessed for colleges and seminaries, spells out much fruitful study. I can rejoice for the future as I have already witnessed denominational and district leadership intuitively understanding and internalizing the principles of assessment and the truths regarding natural talents. These individuals are helping to carry the discovery, application, and training process into the future.

It was at the publication of the *Discovering Your Natural Talents* book, that I met Don and Fred King at the C&MA office in Colorado Springs, and learned of their concern for correctly assessing church planters. Throughout our pilot assessment-training process I encountered many questions from trainees who were steeped in the traditional mystical approach to selecting church planters. They pressed me relentlessly, wanting biblical validation for every principle I taught. Fortunately my previous nineteen years of experience, seminary training with Grant Howard, fine-tuning by Jay Carty, and personal study provided the biblical and logical foundation for my meetings with Don and Fred and the next twenty-five years carving out an assessment process for pastor candidates.

PART III

What Worked

Chapter 4
Buy-In at All Levels

The LORD gives wisdom,
 and from his mouth come knowledge and
understanding. (Proverbs 2:6)

Vision is a picture of the future that produces passion.
Vision is the fuel that leaders run on. It is the fire that
ignites the passion of followers.
—*Bill Hybels,* Courageous Leadership

A tool used is better than a thousand that are not. Many excellent seminar materials gather dust on bookshelves. Unopened software programs sit on thousands of computers. If our assessment process joined that parade, it would have been an utter failure. So the goal was to attain buy-in across the board in the C&MA. Here are just a few of the many benefits that helped sell our people on this assessment process:

This process helped us agree on what to look for in church-planter candidates. A lot was riding on this method for identifying high-potential individuals. We wanted to get it right the first time, and based on our investigation and initial trials, we were convinced that we had found the right solution. The alternative would be to continue by trial-and-error and pay the price.

This process helped us establish a common vocabulary shared by every district leader. Our stewardship of people and resources had previously been hampered by fuzzy and varied terminology. Tackling this problem was a major priority. We needed to work with the same definitions of innate talents and personality traits, to speak the same language in our conversations with one another.

A third benefit: A single unified C&MA process nationwide meant that interview results in one district would be interpreted the same way in all the others. To applicants this would be a huge advantage when interviewing with multiple offices regarding placement. This also saved time for those responsible for placement; they had previously wasted much time repeating assessment procedures and reduplicating efforts.

Related to that, we aimed to empower more pastors to maximize their strengths in established churches. That was an ambitious goal, but considering the potential for increase in healthy ministries, well worth going for. We wanted to ensure that successful pastors would be able to understand the reason for their success, and help them avoid wasting effort in areas where they were not gifted. This also helped in the selection and management of subordinate pastors, who ideally have complementary talents that support the senior pastor.

Finally, we were driven to increase the spiritual fruit in thriving new churches.

At stake were dollars and the mission itself. Reaching spiritually lost people, inviting them to be disciples of Jesus Christ, and forming new healthy churches were of utmost importance. If we could prevent burnout from a pastor overreaching his talent strengths, then we could foster churches that would continue to be grounded and stable.

Carl McGarvey—former director of candidate development at the C&MA national office—was initially skeptical. Now his words reflect the sentiments of many skeptics-become-fans:

> IDAK has given us a wonderful tool to understand our workers and to make better personnel decisions. The common nomenclature and concise definitions help us to communicate accurately as leaders. Not only has it provided us with a marvelous tool, it has provided a framework for training new leaders. We are very grateful for the partnership we enjoy with the IDAK Group.

And district superintendent Jonathan Rich of the Midwest District says this about his enthusiasm for the assessment process:

> Apart from seeing the miracle of new birth radically impact the life a new follower of Jesus, there is little more satisfying in ministry leadership than seeing the light of understanding in a person's eyes as they gain awareness of who God has created them to be. Over the past fifteen years I have used the IDAK assessment tool as a resource enabling me to reveal, confirm, and at times redirect an individual's vocational ministry trajectory. Heart-to-heart conversations like these are always challenging and sometimes extremely difficult. However, the IDAK tool opens transparent conversations devoid of unnecessary emotions and highlights personal discovery through self-awareness. It has been game changer for me.

Contagious Enthusiasm

These passions on the part of C&MA national Church Ministries leaders led to a long-term press for buy-in at every level. In reality, field leadership in a denomination doesn't accept a new initiative or tool simply because it comes down from the national level. The new paradigm has to have innate value that participants come to see for themselves through firsthand exposure. So we took a series of steps to systematically allow all concerned parties to discover the value of this assessment process:

> *The new paradigm has to have innate value that participants come to see for themselves through first-hand exposure.*

Authentication by a Pilot Group

As described earlier, this was a field test to train a half-dozen very active regional leaders. If they gave the thumbs-down, further efforts were doomed. But a thumbs-up would generate momentum. The national office paid the full costs of the training, and IDAK's assessment tools were customized through considerable preparatory work with John Bradley. The results were overwhelmingly positive. Most of the pilot group members bought in to the paradigm and felt it would be worth expanding the training to all district leaders. One who did not buy in, ten years later came around and became one of our greatest advocates.

Improvement through Feedback from the Field

Regional leaders are thoroughly pragmatic. If any proposed program or tool is overly complicated or off target, they will say so. The feedback of our pilot group was extremely important to the shaping of future training modules. Questions, objections, and corrections were welcomed. Each edition of the training incorporated many suggestions for improvement.

Convinced Advocates Who Promoted the Process

This first group of leaders from the field became the promoters to the rest of the district leaders across the U.S. This was the critical factor for two reasons: It validated the process, and it now had advocates outside the national office. It was relatively easy to recruit additional groups for training thereafter.

Two Levels of Training

Typical training seminar formats are designed as one or two days. We realized that the assessment process simply could not be delivered in one short seminar. Participants required initial exposure to the concepts, then time to see them in practice, before continuing with additional training. So from the start, a multiple-phase format was put in place.

Not every district leader had enough interest or motivation to go through the entire course. So we conceded that exposure to the basic principles of the first level would at least equip them with the profiles to look for and the talent terminology. Interestingly, some who initially committed to one level soon saw the program's worth, and returned at their own initiative to take the second level. To ensure quality implementation in all districts, a certification standard was established early in the training process. Each district office was required to have at least one eligible, certified officer to order the testing materials to use with candidates.

Assessment Seminars at Annual District Pastors' Conferences

At least five districts in the early years brought in John Bradley to present the basics of talent assessment at their annual pastors' retreat, thereby reaching a hundred or more pastors per district. These were key points of exposure to a broad group of pastors and church workers. Most superintendents followed up with personal appointments to review each individual's talent profile and discuss the implications. In this way, the IDAK tool became widely known and received favorable reviews.

While I (Don) served as superintendent in Michigan in the late 1990s, nearly every pastor participated in one such seminar. Following up, I took every pastor through a personal review. Most of those sessions led to overwhelmingly positive affirmations of pastors' innate aptitudes and how maximizing these empowered their ministries. That became the platform for many productive follow-up conversations and coaching moments.

There were a couple of tough sessions, though. In one instance, membership in a church had declined drastically—by two thirds in four years—during its current pastor's tenure. Poor relationship dynamics among the church's membership had contributed, but the greater factor seemed to be the pastor's personality. Our session opened the door for me to ask pointed questions about what should be done to address the problem. While he did not like it, I concluded on the basis of his profile and the pattern in the church that he would maximize his talents best by considering either Christian school teaching or the chaplaincy. Eventually he returned to seminary to prepare for a chaplain ministry. He serves to this day as a full-time institutional chaplain.

The greatly weakened church nearly closed. But with membership's agreement, it was placed in the district redevelopment process. With supplementary financial assistance and the arrival of a new pastor with enthusiasm and local roots, it rebounded over the next decade.

Assessment of National Office Department Managers

In the mid-1990s the C&MA's national office HR director encouraged all personnel from the manager level up to undergo a talent assessment to understand the implications personally and for leading their teams. In addition, national office personnel at other levels were recruited to be the trainee clients for district leaders in training. The feedback was overwhelmingly positive, and each training round drew many willing volunteers.

Assessment of College Presidents

District supervisors who were on the boards of the Alliance colleges requested assessment of candidates for the next president. The assessments were highly valued and contributed to making the best placement decisions. In one revealing and sad anecdote, an assessment was performed on a presidential candidate by an Alliance district officer. The candidate who was selected commented that he did not agree with his assessment, but that his strengths were in keeping with the job description. That candidate prevailed with his views and was selected in contradiction to the assessment results. Tragically, his term of office ended early and caused much damage to the campus.

Training on C&MA College Campuses

At the urging of Church Ministries, each of the four colleges opened their doors to training. On some campuses the training was used as a recruitment tool to call out faculty to adopt the curriculum. In other cases, faculty were selected by the president and then attended the IDAK training at the national office. Several years later the office of campus recruitment was developed, which included a representative for each campus. This person was to provide the mentoring and screening of students for pastoral ministry. An attempt was made to develop a four-hour course that could be inserted into an existing class and taught by the campus representative. After a pilot of the course was completed with college students attending at the Crown campus, there still was no follow-through on the part of campus representatives. The lack of follow-through and interest on all five campuses was a big disappointment to both of us. We haven't given up, but this appears to be an uphill effort.

Assessments for Denomination Presidency Candidates

In the 1996 vetting process, the presidential profile was studied from the standpoint of innate talents that would be required. The leading candidates under consideration were interviewed, and the match between their evident talent strengths and the job description was provided to the national nominating committee. That approach was strengthened and broadened in the 2004 search process—five candidates were interviewed to identify the extent of the match, with full profiles given to the committee.

> *Many of the district leaders brought misguided ideas that needed to be considered.*

Developing an assessment process that featured tests and exercises combined with interview validation questions to verify test results had been accomplished. But we still had miles to go as many of the district leaders brought misguided ideas that needed to be considered and addressed.

Made in Heaven

Maybe you're one of the unconvinced. We would urge you to keep reading and give the process a chance. See for yourself how it benefits you. The training continues to be simplified, all assessments are online, and they encourage optimum personal coaching. You might discover something new about yourself or about someone you're guiding into ministry service. You or they might just find the ministry role that God has had waiting since eternity past. The perfect match.

Chapter 5

Starting on the Same Page

The saying is trustworthy: If anyone aspires to the office of overseer [a pastor], he desires a noble task.
(1 Timothy 3:1, ESV)

[When the Bible] outlines church offices, it does not recommend seeking out technically skilled people. There are no suggestions that a leader be a good manager or sharp accountant or even show leadership potential. The essential qualities are spiritual qualities: How committed are they to God? Can they control their temperaments?
—Dr. Paul Brand and Philip Yancey, Fearfully and Wonderfully Made

As mentioned earlier, one of the most formidable barriers we encountered at the start was the lack of consensus on the church-planter qualifications. It was a two-part problem.

First was the lack of a consensus on the needed traits and characteristics. We had lots of ideas floating around, picked up here and there from experts and seminars and books. But they differed significantly. So, not surprisingly, one leader liked this set, while someone else preferred another.

What happened then is that various lists were combined and added to. The compilation stretched longer and longer. It mixed together temperament traits, what we came to know as innate talents, spiritual gifts, and certain desired behaviors. But getting all of the church-planting directors to agree on one list seemed impossible.

Equally challenging, even when leaders did land on a single trait they all found important, there was difficulty defining it. Without an "authorized" dictionary to turn to, each person projected his own perspective.

I (Don) recall a conversation with church-planting leaders before our training that would have been humorous if not so ironic. The group was informally discussing two highly desirable traits in church planters. One was termed "a take-charge leader." Just what was that? Various anecdotes and personal experiences were submitted as definitions. The other trait was termed "a people person." We talked to each other as if everyone knew what that meant too—from personal warmth to going door-to-door in a neighborhood.

> *If we were ever to lift the fog, we had to arrive at a single set of clear definitions.*

Actually we talked *around* both of these terms, circling them with pieces of input and opinion. At the end we established no real clarity, nor a consensus of definition. Each leader walked away with his own pictures. That was the irony: although we had vague ideas of what both traits looked like, we passionately convinced one another that a church planter must possess them!

If we were ever to lift the fog, we had to arrive at a single set of clear definitions. In short, we needed a common vocabulary. It became a high priority to get everyone on the same page.

What we lacked, IDAK's paradigm already had. First, instead of mixing all sorts of traits together, categories had been developed to view them separately. A personality trait is not the same thing as a talent, and the talents need to be differentiated from personal passions. Sorting that out was very helpful.

Second, the list of needed qualifications to be an effective church planter was clearly hammered out. Only nonnegotiables made the cut—a couple of key talent traits and four crucial personality traits, along with spousal agreement and spiritual maturity. We were finally getting somewhere.

Third, each talent and personality trait already had a clear definition drawn from its unique behavioral pattern, which could be observed and identified by a trained interviewer. No more vague, subjective descriptions.

For example, we learned that it was not enough to have the candidate affirm that he or she was "a people person" or to read that on a reference form. Instead, it was much more precise to identify how quickly that person established relational bonds with new acquaintances. Those who naturally did that within minutes or hours, repeatedly, even when meeting strangers, demonstrated a Multi-Relational talent. Observing this pattern of behavior *outside* of a work environment, where it would be an expected skill, was the key to affirming its presence. The importance of this innate ability in a church planter should be obvious even in all other types of social settings.

It surprised me how quickly we advanced toward consensus. Before long we had the common vocabulary so greatly needed. Not only did the content of conversations about church planters sharpen as the new standardized terminology was adopted, but the validity of our selection process increased.

The importance of being on the same page cannot be overstated.

The Six Suitcases

One of the sad yet common practices that I (John) noticed among some leaders wanting to accurately access new hires was the use of testing instruments based upon a simplified formula of four or more different profile descriptions (the sanguine, the rancher, ENTJ, and so on). Sadly, these assessments cannot be validated by interview, nor were they initially conceived from a biblical view of men and women and their work. If the presupposition of a testing instrument is that a person can acquire skills for most any type of work as long as they have proper self-discipline, intelligence, and motivation, then all one has to test for is self-discipline, intelligence, and motivation. This philosophical view negates the role of a sovereign God who has indeed gifted men and women with specific skills that enable them to do certain things exceedingly well. This also means that the same God has chosen to withhold certain skills from each person.

Now, if a student has decided he wants to be a pastor, his approach to his education could be to gain the skills needed in order to pastor. And further, if he aspired to be a church planter, he would seek to acquire those skills as well. The history of the Alliance has proven this logic false. One cannot will his way to acquiring skills that God didn't give him. It's simply not biblically possible for the foot to become an eye, no matter how much it might want to (1 Corinthians 12:15-25). Another way of saying this is, pursuing someone else's path may lead to your dead end.

> *One cannot will his way to acquiring skills that God didn't give him.*

We need a method for distinguishing between qualities that can and cannot be attained without God's prior gifting. For example, we can all choose to grow in honesty, but we can't all become concert pianists. Therefore to help provide a set of categories for understanding one's attributes, skills, gifts, and talents, the paradigm of the *six suitcases* was developed.

#1   #2   #3   #4   #5   #6

#1 *The Work and Volunteer Case*

This suitcase contains your life-journey skills learned "on the job." It includes all the hands-on-related tasks you have carried out, from the first lawn mowing or babysitting job all the way up to your present career position. Some of these jobs are not salaried positions, such as home responsibilities, volunteer work, or community service. Some are routine jobs (for example, household chores); others may occur only once in your life (for example, lead role in a dramatic presentation). This suitcase contains the "I have done ..." statements.

An interesting client case study illustrates how many of us assume that one's occupational learned skills represent one's innate talents. I recall Larry, who as a retired mechanical engineer with a doctoral degree could find no mission board to accommodate his desire to serve as a missionary. Over and over he was told, "We have no positions for a doctorate in mechanical engineering." After we completed his assessment, we discovered several talent strengths, one of which was Researching. I suggested that he introduce himself as one whom God had gifted with the talent of Researching. Several weeks later I was speaking to a group of mission recruiters about the importance of talents. I mentioned that a retired professional had the talent of Researching and wanted to serve in missions. Several hands went up. These agencies indicated that they could definitely use that talent; the person's work experience was secondary or even immaterial to them.

#2 The School Case

The second suitcase holds your life-journey education and training achievements. It's filled with your knowledge skills. You acquire these through formal education, informal reading, attending lectures or conferences, or conducting your own YouTube research. This suitcase contains the "I have a degree in ..." and "I know about ..." statements.

#3 The Temperament/Personality Case

The third suitcase is filled with the inner qualities of your life—character, disposition, sociability characteristics. These contents combine the raw material that God put in you, which I call a predisposed proclivity that is part of your DNA. About 30 percent of each of your temperament traits are hardwired. The remaining source of your temperament or personality comes from your family conditioning, your community culture, your spiritual environment, your network of friends, and your own self-discipline.

Notice that you have less immediate selection and control of the contents of this case compared to the first two suitcases. When people describe themselves according to these qualities, they tend to incorrectly assume certain unchangeable, lifelong patterns in their makeup. Several psychological and personality tests, such as the Myers-Briggs and the DISC, are popular for categorizing behavioral patterns within each type. People characterize themselves by saying, "I am a type-A personality," or "I am choleric," or "I am direct-expressive," or "I am an ENTJ." One only needs to refer to the book of Proverbs to see that we are all encouraged to model certain temperament traits, such as the self-discipline of an ant, regardless of our innate proclivity. This suitcase contains many (but certainly not all) of your "I am the type of person who ..." statements.

From our study of pastoral works, we identified thirty-two temperament traits, dividing them into two categories—five primary traits, including Character, Self-Esteem, Self-Discipline, Optimism, and Team Player, which were determined to be essential; and twenty-seven secondary traits that are worth consideration only if they appear to be extremely unfavorable.

#4 The Interests Case

The fourth suitcase contains interests, attractions, and fascinations that you have collected and continue to collect in your life's journey. Some of these are with you and others have passed.

Here we're examining your taste in food and music, your recreation and hobbies, your entertainment, your attraction to certain colors, and anything else that delights you. You might talk of the thrill of riding roller-coasters, the adventure of travel, or the challenge of flying an airplane. This suitcase combined with the next one, the values case, comprises the bulk of your motivation, your vision, your passion.

This fourth suitcase is a rather large one. It is continually expanding with new contents as you are exposed to new potential interests. It contains the "I like ..." statements.

#5 The Values Case

In the fifth suitcase you carry all that is important to you, now and in the future of your life's journey. These are deep-seated convictions and commitments. This is what you esteem, prize, and regard—the things you consider worthy, significant, or of consequence. These values guide the decisions you make—the ingredients of the food you eat, the movies you do and don't watch, and the justice you champion. Your basis for marriage and parenting, your Christian beliefs, the attitude you have toward God's Word—all of these fit into your values case.

This case is not as large as your interests case because it does not add or lose items as quickly. Normally it involves a gradual growing process. However, when there is a major change in your life—such as death of a loved one, divorce, major illness or injury, or job loss—you may reevaluate and adjust your values more sharply.

Combined with the interests suitcase, this represents a powerful foundation for one's heart-passion drives, affecting such important life pursuits as selecting a career goal, developing a work ethic, determining what is a fair wage, wanting certain employment health benefits, and the like.

An unfortunate trap in choosing one's life calling is to choose based solely on one's interests and values, ignoring one's talents in the final suitcase.

#6 The Talents Case

The talents case is often ignored or forgotten, if one assumes that he or she can acquire most any skill needed to excel in a job. This suitcase does not eclipse the significance of the other five. They are all important. But the talents are unavoidable as the hardwiring that God selected to be part of each one of us when He created us. A person's circumstances and upbringing are irrelevant—whether adoption, a dysfunctional home, or alcoholism—his or her natural talents are still intact, the way God gave them at birth. Of course, to excel in the application of one's talents, one must develop them and continue to hone and polish them until a level of mastery is achieved.

IDAK has identified fifty-four talents as uniquely innate, God-given. The appendix provides an alphabetical list of all of these talent traits and their definitions, along with a separate list of talents that best correlate with pastoral job duties.

The Taxonomy of Talents

Since 1973 I (John) have been formally studying natural talents to determine which are God-given and innate, as opposed to personal qualities that can be acquired by hard work or education. Through a process that has involved three doctoral dissertations, my colleagues and I have identified a total of fifty-four natural talents and validated those through over 90,000 career options. We have classified these talents into three categories: Communicational, Relational, and Functional (task-oriented traits). When sharing the essence of natural talents in seminars, I use the illustration of the atomic elements that we learned about in high school chemistry. The elements are the root or core of a particle. Each element has clear distinctives that are the same wherever applied. When elements are combined, they form a molecule, such as the common H_2O molecule for water. This is also true about talents. Each has its unique disposition regardless of where (in whom) it is found. When combined with other talents and personality qualities, the aggregate forms a person's unique identity.

The first classification of talents are those that represent Communicational distinctives (see the appendix for a detailed list of natural talents). Our team has identified fifteen distinctly unique traits for this category. No one person has all; each person has at least one and a maximum of three as innate strengths. Normally, we tend to classify most people into two categories—good communicators (politicians, salespeople, teachers, marketers) and not-good communicators (mechanics, accountants, bus drivers, and others who are usually not good with words). But in Scripture, God indicates that He has created all to be good communicators, if for no reason other than that all are called to communicate their faith. But not everyone communicates in the same way. Surprisingly, six of the fifteen are nonverbal Communicational talents. These are commonly referred to as modes of artistic and musical expression. The statement is true: "A picture is worth a thousand words." Handel, who wrote *The Messiah*, has shared the full gospel with millions, yet without ever preaching a sermon, leading a Bible study, or even having a conversation with the receivers of his message.

For pastors there is one most preferred talent of the fifteen: Giving Speeches (or preaching). This talent is also referred to as the *pulpit* trait. There is an acceptable second-place talent for the pulpit: Teaching. And even a third: Writing, combined with Acting, commonly referred to as *dramatic reading*—reading one's sermon with dramatic flair. And yes, a B-plus talent for preaching will also work. There are misguided attempts to twist the Giving Presentations talent into a pulpit talent. This only frustrates and stresses the pastor and has less than desirable results in the congregation. Therefore in order to succeed as a pastor, one has to be "good" in the pulpit. In fact, any job that requires frequent public speaking is a natural fit for the individual who is gifted with the Speeches (Preaching) talent.

A second classification of talents is the Relational category. This group represents the various ways of forming trust bonds with others. In order to share our faith, it is important to first establish a credible trust bond with another. The three Relational talents vary with the length of time it takes to form this trust bond. Some form a trust bond within minutes or hours

(Multi-Relational). These are the most popular and well-liked youth in high school. Wherever they go, they make deep friendships quickly and easily. More important, they get a boost of energy when they form a new friendship. A second and more common Relational talent normally forms trust bonds over a nine- to twelve-month period (Familiar Group Relational). Lastly, the third talent forms very deep trust bonds, but it takes three or more years to do so (Singular Relational). If one were to select the talent for one's personal discipler, the best choice would be the third; you would be one of the most important people to that disciple maker, who forms few, but very deep relationships.

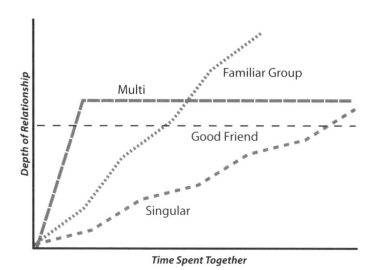

Relational Talents

All three of these Relational traits can apply to pastoral ministry. (Multi- and Familiar Group Relational talents are best suited to church planting.) The third, however, requires a strong pulpit strength in order to quickly gain the trust and respect of the congregation, since relationship-based bonds take a long time for this person. Many famous past and present preachers represent this Singular Relational talent.

A last classification of talents is the Functional category. This third category includes the task-oriented behavioral aptitudes, the doing-something talents. In this group we find important talents that determine the unique approach to ministry a candidate may take. Among the thirty-six talents in this group, several are more favored for a successful pastorate. However, there is considerable latitude among these talents.

A cluster of three talents in this group are labeled the Supervisory talents (Initiating/Developing, Long-Range Planning, and Managing). This means that each brings to the job the capacity to oversee and coordinate the activities of others. When attempting to predict the congregation size that a pastor candidate will be able to lead, one of these Supervisory talents is needed in order to grow a church beyond three hundred or so members.

Knowing all the talents and their application to pastoral positions was key. Yet we needed to address issues of how talents related to the call of God for church planters.

Chapter 6
Ministry-Impacting Distinctions

Do not lay hands on anyone too hastily.
(1 Timothy 5:22, NASB)

Consistent with Scripture and with two thousand years of
church history, the community of faith typically affirms
functional callings through the local church. ... When God
calls a person into a functional ministry, the body of Christ
confirms that calling.
—*Dr. George M. Hillman,* Ministry Greenhouse

I (John) recall a bittersweet church-plant client story. Frank was working in veterinary medicine after graduation. His church issued a call to plant a church in a certain African village, and he in particular was encouraged to consider going. After much prayer and the urging of his friends, he left his practice and moved to that village to begin evangelistic and church-planting work. He was so committed that he even married a woman from the village.

Sadly, the work never got off the ground. After seven years he returned home feeling like a failure. A few months later, he came to my office to talk about what he should do for the next chapter of his life. His assessment results confirmed his initial choice of veterinarian; they did not confirm his passion to be a church planter, nor even to engage in any cross-cultural interaction.

As I listened to his story and then prepared the summary reports, I proposed the following scenario to him: "What if you had gone to the very same village as a veterinarian willing to serve the needs of the tribe's animal herds. After about three years, wouldn't you reasonably expect to have earned their trust and respect? With this relational bond, couldn't you have invited church planters from your church to come over and begin the process of winning souls and building the foundation of a church?" He looked at me with an amazed stare. That would have been so simple. His energies could have been productively redirected if he had gone through this assessment *before* embarking on his quest. It doesn't take much imagination to see how the end of the story could have been different if Frank had focused on his natural talents first, rather than just run with his passion.

The Hunt for Gifted Church Planters

We have discussed in other chapters the unique Functional talent that is critical for a successful new start church plant. That talent is Initiating/Developing. We further classified this talent in a group identified as the Supervisory talents—three talents that bring the innate capacity to oversee and coordinate the activities of others. The church-planting talent is also referred to as the *visionary* talent or the *entrepreneur* talent. The talent brings to the job the innate ability to cast forth a compelling vision and to recruit others to that vision, holding their feet to the fire until the startup phase is completed.

Church planters need more than just the Initiating/Developing talent. They must also be strong in the pulpit, thereby delivering a compelling weekly sermon that will draw individuals to come week after week. As one starts to itemize the important traits, one quickly finds that truly qualified candidates will be extremely rare. Not only must one be a gifted entrepreneur, but one also must be able to communicate his faith in a compelling way, possessing as well a host of other traits. A denomination that wants to gather as many gifted church planters as possible should consider these options:

a. Recruit talented students early in college, rather than waiting for them to volunteer.

b. Recruit second-career men and women.

c. Plant daughter churches that do not require the Initiator/Developer talent.

The Call in Terms of Natural Talents

Too many times I (John) have listened to frustrated district superintendents remark how difficult it is to challenge a candidate when he says, "God has called me to pastoral ministry." And then I hear, "Who am I to question one's calling?" I faced this problem head on when I was invited to teach at seminary and Bible college classes in vocational training schools preparing students for ministry service. Just how was I to explain the facts to a passionate student who claimed he was called when it was obvious he lacked the talents needed for pastoral ministry? Fortunately, my study of God's Word provided a model that has succeeded in explaining this thorny issue.

When teaching, I will draw three circles overlapping in the middle. The circle on top I label, "The Prompting of God." Biblical references like Moses and the burning bush, Paul on the road to Damascus, and the prophet Samuel as a young intern testify that God sometimes actively prompts His saints to move in the direction of ministry service.

The circle to the right I label, "The Community's Confirmation." (Don will discuss this further in a moment.)

The third and last circle on the left side I label, "Suited Natural Talents." Since these aptitudes are God-given, it is reasonable to assume that God has expectations that the person will use them in his or her life calling.

When all three circles overlap in the middle—the alignment of God's prompting, the community's confirmation, and God's equipping—this makes for a solid calling. This then can be verified by a district before making a placement decision.

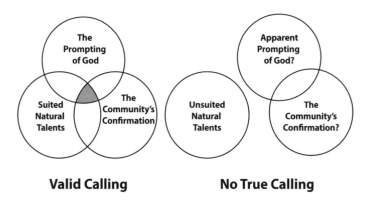

Valid Calling   **No True Calling**

More on the Community's Confirmation

I (Don) would like to expand on one component of John's preceding model before moving on.

By its very nature, assessment involves making discerning decisions about where a candidate's natural talents indicate he or she can best serve the Lord. However, a longstanding argument contradicts the very basis of this assumption. It goes like this: Those whom God calls, God will equip.

For example, when individuals claim a divine call to a specific type of ministry—church planting or cross-cultural missions—well-meaning friends, pastors, or other leaders may assure them that God will equip them with whatever they lack. Whether it is a needed language-learning aptitude or cultural adaptability, the new worker can expect to receive such enablement, having said yes to the call.

Placement leaders have been known to accept this claim even if they do not see evidence in the candidate of aptitudes for a specialized task. Believing either that new gifts will be given at the entry point, or that passion and hard work will compensate, they override an assessment that points in a different direction.

To some, this fallacy becomes a firm spiritual conviction. Placement should be made on the basis of a passionate testimony to a divine call, they reason. "Real faith" is believing that God's equipping will follow. Such belief asserts that, in contrast, human assessment methods lead to "unspiritual" human opinions about a candidate. Putting faith in those assessment results shows a lack of faith.

This argument has been repeated so often by so many for so long that some have given it the credibility of Holy Scripture. Questioning it seems like an offense to God Himself. But is it true?

There is no doubt that God calls individuals to certain ministries. The Bible reveals many instances where He sovereignly chose someone to be a prophet, or a king, or an apostle. And He did indeed work powerfully within them, even the reluctant ones, to accomplish His plan. That we celebrate and do not debate.

However, consider additional discoveries in the New Testament that need to be taken into account.

In the early days after Pentecost, the church in Jerusalem experienced explosive growth. To manage the daily food distribution fairly to the growing number of disciples, the apostles ordered the responsibility to be given to a seven-man team. Interestingly, the basis for selection was "men...who are *known to be* full of the Holy Spirit *and* wisdom" (Acts 6:3, emphasis added). It was not enough to be Spirit-filled; it was also necessary to be wise. The two characteristics complemented one another. And each was discernible by—probably even obvious to—the community of Jesus' followers. They presented seven to the apostles, who prayed and then commissioned them with the laying on of hands.

> *It was not enough to be Spirit-filled; it was also necessary to be wise.*

Another interesting selection is found in Acts 13. During a time of worship and fasting by the prophets and teachers in the Antioch church, "the Holy Spirit said, 'Set apart for me Barnabas and Saul for the work to which I have called them'" (13:2). Here is the divine call. Notice also the context in which the Spirit spoke. He issued the call among and to the community of church leaders. Neither Barnabas nor Paul came to the leaders with an independent claim to have been called. The leaders received the announcement. And then, in response, they took more time to confirm what the Spirit had told them: They fasted and prayed, then "placed their hands on [Barnabas and Saul] and sent them off" (13:3). Prayer, fasting, blessing, and sending are all mentioned. This, we would argue, is evidence of the pattern of human confirmation of the divine call.

However, the most obvious example is the selection of elders (and deacons) in the New Testament era. Though Paul commended the desire to serve as an overseer in the church (1 Timothy 3:1), passion to lead was not enough. He stated that "the overseer must be" a person who demonstrated definite spiritual maturity and character qualities. He set up a detailed standard, no doubt for the sake of purity and consistency in all the new churches.

Evidently, not only the apostle Paul was able to discern those who had such qualities. His associate Titus, having been left on the island of Crete, was specifically charged to "appoint elders in every town" where there was a church (Titus 1:5). The appointments were made according to the same standard that Paul established elsewhere (1:6-9).

The point is that the practice of human discernment and discretion by Spirit-filled leaders, to be sure, is not contradictory to the reality of an individual's divine call to vocational ministry. In fact, we argue that the two are complementary.

Based on early church accounts, we would put forth a revised truism: Those whom God calls, God affirms through the leaders of the ministry. We believe a complementary approach is best. It fully acknowledges—even expects—the divine initiative of the Spirit to call persons into ministry. But the belief of a divine call is not wholly dependent on the subjective experience of one person or couple. It is the responsibility of the spiritual leaders around them, who know them, to affirm their calling. If a call is valid, it can and will be affirmed by responsible spiritual leaders over time.

Alongside divine initiative, a complementary approach also respects the careful evaluation of wise and mature leaders in the church. "Do not lay hands on anyone too hastily," Paul says (1 Timothy 5:22, NASB). And deacons "must first be tested; and then if there is nothing against them, let them serve" (3:10).

During a mission conference some years ago in a church where I (Don) served, a young couple responded to the missionary's passionate appeal to take the gospel into unreached areas of the world. However, there was an obvious hurdle in front of them. The husband had a severe speech impediment that made verbal communication difficult.

Two church elders were asked to meet with the couple about their call. I believe they gave godly counsel. Neither elder disputed the couple. Instead they suggested that if God wanted them to learn to speak another language, the husband should earnestly pray for healing from his impediment while getting a diagnosis by a speech therapist. And yes, the elders anointed and prayed for him and volunteered to cover the cost of therapy.

By handling the situation with grace and wisdom, they truly helped this young couple. For several months the husband did pray, and he obtained a professional diagnosis. Following a course of speech therapy, he came to realize that the spiritual burden he felt was legitimate. And he also came to terms with the long-term limitations of his disability, from which he had not been healed. In the end, he determined to do all in his present sphere of influence to be a witness until or unless the Lord Jesus divinely healed him. This was a rather dramatic example of the complementary approach that employs both wisdom and practical assessment.

Norming the Psych Profile

In addition to discovering the power of innate talents, we also needed to find out if there were common personality traits among the most successful C&MA pastors. These norms would help us screen for the presence of traits that are crucial for church planters and workers seeking insight. But we encountered a problem.

Psychological tests rely on general population averages, or *norms*, to set the parameters of what is considered normal. These norms are not static, but change over time. For example, take the Taylor-Johnson trait of Hostility versus Tolerance. Which way is the change moving in our culture? Definitely toward more tolerance. Thus, the threshold of what is considered a hostile temperament trait moves lower and lower. Measured against this changing norm, Christians who believe in moral absolutes will show up as increasingly hostile.

About twenty years ago, the psychological test, 16PF introduced its fourth edition, based on an updated general population norm. At that same time, John was conducting a training event at the Alliance national office that included talent and temperament assessment for about fifty managers. He used the new fourth edition. Much to John's and Don's surprise, the test results placed the majority of the national office managers as right-wing extremists. Something had to be done.

To overcome this problem, we needed to develop psychological scoring norms for our own workers. We began by asking Alliance superintendents to select fifty established pastors and their wives, who they felt were successful. And also select fifty church planters that they felt had succeeded in planting a thriving church. We had each group of pastors complete the 16PF psychological assessment instrument. We contracted with Dr. Neal McBride, a psychometrics professor who taught at George Fox University's psychology program and later at Azuza University. We sent him the scored profiles. He then processed the scores, looking for any significant deviations from the general population norm. It was no surprise that the pastors and their wives showed a significant deviation in several areas from the general population. Church planters also showed an additional significant deviation from the more traditional pastors.

These adjusted scores were then used as more suitable norms when reporting the test results of Alliance pastor candidates. Ten years later, the process was completed again with Dr. McBride, this time norming two tests, adding the Taylor Johnson Temperament Analysis along with the 16PF to our test group. As before, we found a significant number of traits to be significantly and statistically different from the general population norm, so these became part of our new standard for measuring effective

As before, we found a significant number of traits to be significantly and statistically different from the general population norm.

pastors and church planters. We were then able to "compare apples with apples," matching our candidates more successfully against the right targets—true profiles of successful pastors or church planters.

Assessment at College and Seminary Levels

The reality hit us that our desire to plant and grow many more healthy churches, and to send out new cross-cultural workers internationally, would never come into being unless we raised the numbers in the candidate pipeline. We had to start identifying potential ministry candidates earlier.

Coinciding with that reality was another development. The C&MA student ministry leaders have for decades put on a triennial high school student event called LIFE Conference. The pinnacle of that event is a public appeal to the five to seven thousand students to yield themselves wholly to God and to volunteer to be available for His service.

By the late 1990s and in the early 2000s, the appeals received an incredible surge of responses—over six hundred students completed commitment cards at one LIFE public service. Each responding student was followed up and encouraged to prepare for ministry at one of the four Alliance colleges across the U.S.

Merely waiting until they graduated was not enough. So the denomination responded. Funds were reallocated to enlarge the staff or the Candidate Development Office. A C&MA representative was appointed to each campus. The primary purpose was to recruit potential ministry candidates and to shepherd them through the preparation process. The dream was to implement a true development process for students through the campus representatives, who received assessment training that would be a major component of their guidance work.

Success at this phase was spotty. The assessment paradigm was not embraced fully by regional personnel. However, that office has recently been reorganized and new representatives are in place. We are prepared to make another run at helping them build a strong preparation track for ministry applicants.

We urge all appropriate district leaders and educators to take this opportunity seriously and to support it as you are able. Not only will you play a key role in guiding gifted church planters toward the destiny for which God has equipped them, but *all* students who undergo assessment and guidance will benefit by gaining valuable self-knowledge and using their years of training in focused preparation for the tasks for which they are best suited.

What is more, if a student tests as a freshman and discovers a problematic temperament trait, such as high Hostility (which, unlike talent traits, can be improved upon with focused self-discipline), then the student and the school have four years in which to work specifically on that problem area, providing an even more solid foundation and increasing the likelihood of a learned containment of the hostility when the graduate enters ministry. This student and all the thousands he or she will touch will have you to thank for preventing much avoidable frustration, failure, and pain in his or her ministry.

Considering Alternate Ministry Options

The initial purpose of our assessment process was to identify church-planter candidates. That meant that some fit the profile and some didn't. In that regard, our process in the early days resembled the typical pass/fail "test." And, frankly, not many proved well-suited for church planting.

So what to do with all the others? Once again, this question sprang from a conviction to steward the people God gives to oversee His church. We could not simply leave so many with a sense that they did not measure up. And, after all, each ministry candidate was looking for guidance, regardless.

Superintendents, too, were eager to apply the process to a broader pool of candidates, since so much of their placement work is with existing churches. So we set out to expand our ability to provide affirming guidance for every candidate bought into the assessment process at the district level. Fortunately, it was possible to customize the IDAK tools to expand our applications. Separate profiles were drawn up for lead pastors—both in solo situations and in those with multiple staff—and for various staff positions. The profiles were validated, and then subsequent training rounds included how to identify the key talent strengths in all of the now-available profiles. Armed with this additional knowledge, our people in the field were able to assess candidates for a variety of ministry leadership roles.

I (Don) personally have found these wider applications have taken my personnel work to an entirely new level. A few years ago, a former professional baseball player came to me on the recommendation of a mutual friend. After his baseball career ended, Pete had joined the staff of a megachurch, taking charge of leadership of a large men's ministry. However, a new lead pastor came along and in the transition, Pete was let go. Now in his mid-forties, he was full of questions about what to do next, mixed with more than a little self-doubt about his abilities.

After we met for an introductory session, in which he unpacked his story and shared his confusion about his future, I sent him home to complete the Career Match assessment. A few weeks later we met again for the autobiographical interview and results interpretation. At first Pete had a difficult time not straying into self-promoting claims of his abilities, as if he needed to prove himself or pass some kind of pass/fail test. Once we got beyond that point, the time became productive.

I explained the value of building his future ministry responsibilities around his God-given abilities. The lights went on for Pete. He reflected on the parts of his previous ministry that were draining for him—notably organizing and "desk duties." "I need to be active and engaging with people," he told me.

Besides Physical Coordination—an obvious talent for an athlete—I saw evidence of an A-plus-level talent for Promoting. Not arrogant self-promotion, but the ability to persuade others to accept new and different viewpoints. Pete obviously had the natural enthusiasm and excitement that often accompanies the exercise of this talent.

Promoting, combined with a Multi-Relational talent and a Giving Presentations talent, gave Pete tremendous potential for positions in the church or the nonprofit world that would require him to be the "front man" or public relations face for a new or existing ministry that needed a fresh injection of excitement and motivation. As we explored that direction, he mentioned the nonprofit ministry of another Christian ex-professional athlete he knew and admired.

"Go talk to him!" I said. "Network with him and his contacts. That's the ideal setting for you. Check out if they have a role that you know now you would fit."

Since I don't do direct placement outside of church and church-related ministry, that was as far as I could go with Pete. We prayed together for God's guidance to a position that fit Pete well, in which he would thrive. He left our session with his spirits lifted, knowing better how to steward God's gifts.

Less than a year later we ran into each other. Pete thanked me for the clarification and encouragement. He had found a position just like the one we discussed! Talk about satisfaction. A brother who could have wallowed in discouragement and confusion was instead pointed along a path that led to a great fit and fulfillment in ministry.

We were well on our way to completing our assessment process. One further step required that we focus on the candidate interviewing process and the key role of the district officer in making the final evaluation decision.

Chapter 7
Assessing the Whole Person

*The best managers identify the talents that are needed for
a particular position and then find people who fit the role.
This means looking beyond a person's knowledge and skills
to size up whether a job really "fits" the person.*
—Senior Vice President Curt Coffman, The Gallup
Organization, quoted in SHRM News

You created my inmost being;
        you knit me together in my mother's womb.
I praise you because I am fearfully and wonderfully made.
(Psalm 139:13-14)

When King David wrote this beautiful expression of adoration
to God the Creator, he was deeply conscious that who and what
he was found its origin in God's creative design. We can draw
from this passage that each of us is a like a tapestry, intricately
woven by the Master Weaver. And each person is unique and
multifaceted, a one-of-a-kind masterpiece.

A significant foundation of the practical theology of assessment is the belief that no test devised by humans can serve

as the ultimate truth about a person's hardwiring. The innate gifting of a person can be misdiagnosed no matter how targeted the testing system. Human beings are so wondrously made that no test can serve as the ultimate truth about a person's hardwiring. The totality of a person's inner gifting cannot be fully revealed, no matter how valid the instrument. That realization causes us to pause and recognize our limitations. It leads us to approach each assessment with humility, recognizing that we dare not pontificate about another person's shortcomings.

> *No test devised by man can serve as the ultimate truth about a person's hardwiring.*

Instead, we take into account the incredible variety of individuals God has made, respecting His creativity. If we fail to do that, we can be too simplistic and overlook some important facet of the human makeup. So when we assess the complexities of personhood, we know that it should be executed with a humble spirit.

A recent client story helps illustrate how each of us is uniquely fashioned. Jim came to me (John) quite disillusioned. He was adamant that God had called him to be a teacher in missions. He pointed to numerous experiences where he sensed the Spirit of God moving him toward that occupation. He was educated as an electrical engineer and felt the calling into full-time ministry about five years into his profession. He quit his job and enrolled to acquire a teaching credential. He then applied to a mission agency, which appointed him to a school overseas. The first year was very stressful—so much so that he resigned. He tried several other mission teaching opportunities, all of them failures.

Returning to the U.S., he needed income, so he went back to his engineering profession. A little while later we met. His assessment revealed a very interesting profile. Among many talent strengths, Teaching was surprisingly missing. Zero. Not even a blip on the chart. But how, he asked, could God have called him to do something that God had not gifted him to do? One of his talent strengths was Tutoring. The talent definition for Tutoring includes patiently assisting someone who is unable to understand the curriculum by himself or herself—for example, those who are autistic, have ADHD, or are mentally challenged. Tutoring is in the Helping talent family—suggesting a coming-alongside-and-nurturing type of role.

As we began to research people groups he might serve, we discovered a deep passion—packed away in his values suitcase—for the marginalized, the underdog, the forgotten, the slow. I asked if he would be willing to consider teaching challenging students? And so he launched into a new, fulfilling direction for his life. We were able to redeem his passion to serve in a teaching role, but in a different manner from what he had originally considered.

Any given individual is amazingly complex. Assessment and direction is not always a slam dunk. It requires the careful assessment of a coach who knows all the variables and truly believes in stewardship of God's people.

The Supplemental Behavioral Interview

The assessment system we have used places the final evaluation in the hands of the assessment officer. This person has been appointed to this important role and therefore should have the authority to make his or her own judgment once all the information has been considered. To empower the officer, the assessment process supplies him or her with validation questions that focus on a candidate's past behavioral patterns. These validation questions should carry more weight than the written test results in determining a candidate's fitness for duty.

Since the talent of Initiating/Developing is the key trait for church planter, let's use that as an example of the interview validation process. The questions below are designed to identify the Initiating/Developing talent in a church-planting pastor candidate.

1. In your assessment results, you have selected the talent Initiating/Developing as a strength. Could you define that talent in your own words?

2. Could you give three recent examples when you used that talent?

3. Did you run for any offices in high school, college, or youth group? Why or why not? What was the result of your term in office? (The interviewer is looking for statements such as, "I started ..." or "I saw a need and convinced a group of students ...")

4. Once you lead others in a startup project, how long does it take before you lose interest? Give examples. (An Initiator/Developer usually last two years and then loses interest unless there are additional issues to champion.)

5. Recall leadership roles that did not bring out the best in you and other roles that did. What made the difference? Give three examples. (Generally an Initiator/Developer manifests frustration with others who give up too quickly, who are not willing to put their feet to the fire and persevere.)

The same process is used when seeking to validate a candidate's temperament trait, such as Character.

1. Please define Character in your own words.

2. Give three examples of significant trials when you paid a price for your faith.

3. What is the most costly decision you have made? How would you make that decision today?

4. Are there unexpected trials others have experienced regarding their faith that caused you to think about your response if that were to happen to you?

5. Have you experienced any emergency crossroads in your faith journey when there was an easy option versus a more difficult option for you? Please explain.

By supplementing the assessment test exercise results with these biographical questions about events of the past, the interviewer can gain his own perspective regarding a trait in order to make a final informed decision. One of the features of the assessment process was to use the validation questions as part of an initial conversation with a prospective candidate over lunch. We termed the process "Doing an assessment on a napkin."

Differentiating Talents from Work Experience and Education

One of the most difficult assessment hurdles is to set aside a person's occupational history and seminary degree and look deep within to determine their hardwired strengths. The mistaken logic goes something like this: If a candidate has fifteen years of pastoral experience, isn't it reasonable to expect that he has strengths in preaching, relating to people, managing others, getting tasks done on time, leading board meetings, training for evangelism, and the like?

Rather than working to discredit this natural approach to candidate assessment, we featured the six suitcases paradigm. By explaining that a person has valuable work experience skills and skills learned through education, we acknowledged the value of one's resume history. However, we then explained that even though a person has experience doing something, this doesn't mean that he is gifted by God for those activities. Our goal is maximum productivity, not marginal or adequate productivity. Just being okay at pastoring was not acceptable.

We then followed with the vision question: What if this candidate could be a master craftsman in a different leadership role? Wouldn't you want to open him to that possibility? Wouldn't the denomination benefit with more leaders in their sweet spots rather than just pastors plugging along in mediocrity? Doesn't God deserve better than C-plus or even B-plus performance?

> *Even though a person has experience doing something, this doesn't mean that he is gifted by God for those activities.*

I (Don) have come to understand the importance of looking far deeper than the claim, implied on resumes, that certain educational degrees and types of ministry experience are the most significant credentials for future placement. Candidates are not to be blamed for believing this claim. Conventional wisdom asserts if you have the degree and some experience in the associated field, then you are prepared to climb the ladder to larger roles. This assumption is often built into a resume.

However, a person is much more than his or her education and work experience, and these additional dimensions must be explored. I call it "going beyond the paper" to the person. I think most people who hire or make placement decisions know this. But not everyone knows what specific questions to ask or how to probe.

Learning about a person's talents and temperament through our assessment process has added the missing dimensions. Nothing is foolproof, but we have greatly strengthened the basis for understanding our candidates and giving them wise counsel based on the way God has designed them. This approach has the advantage of going far beyond the typical interaction with a candidate over his or her resume. It provides the basis for making wise placement decisions. And it enhances our stewardship of the applicant.

Differentiating Talents from Temperament Traits

During our training seminars, as we introduced the model with natural talents as the bedrock traits that define a person's leadership role, we were repeatedly asked, "What about personality traits? Where do they fit in?" Many of the district officers had been using personality assessment instruments, such as the Myers Briggs, the DISC, and the TJTA. Some officers had a prior background in counseling, and one was a psychologist. We also came to realize that talented candidates carried emotional baggage; some had mental health issues.

We responded to these important questions by returning to the foundation paradigm, the six suitcases. Temperament or personality traits are identified as a separate suitcase of traits, yet also noted under the "hardwired" category, meaning God-given.

Yet there is an important distinction in understanding these traits. Most psychologists agree that one's personality is partially determined by their gene code (approximately 30 percent), and partially by their positive or negative environment as they grow up, through the influence of parents, school, peers, church, and faith (70 percent). In addition, the 70 percent is influenced by the positive role of the Holy Spirit within the believer.

This important part of pastoral assessment gave rise to identifying key temperament or personality traits that were determined to be essential for peak job performance, as well as traits that would point a candidate toward a different role. In addition to these top primary traits, a host of secondary traits could be problematic if found to be excessively abnormal (see appendix).

The biblical perspective that helped me understanding how temperament traits apply to ministry leadership was in Ephesians 4, where Paul admonishes the Christian to no longer walk as gentiles walk—that is, to put off the old man—and to be renewed—that is, to put on the new man. Paul then lists several improper old man habits that are to be put away, such as lying, wrath, stealing, using corrupt words, and so on. I reasoned that the command to put on the new man and to stop behaving inappropriately presupposes that a Christian has the ability to do this if he or she sets his or her mind to do so. In short, a Christian can and should clean up one's act. For ministry leaders, Paul's standard of new man behavior is even higher, found in 1 Timothy 3 and Titus 1. The assessment process, then, attempts to determine how well one has followed Paul's admonition to clean up one's act.

Take Anger, for example, defined as High Intolerance, a secondary temperament trait in the MAX Report. Most would agree that a candidate inclined to excessive hostility could be eliminated from the selection process. Let's go one step further. If a person is born with a proclivity toward anger, yet he learns by effective parenting and/or teaching and the inner working of the Holy Spirit how to control it, this person should get a pass on that trait even if the psychological testing identified his anger was above normal. This self-control of anger's hurtful outbursts is what Paul referred to in Ephesians 4:26: "Be angry and yet do not sin" (NASB).

In addition to Ephesians, I also learned from Proverbs that certain personality traits—laziness, excessive anger, and the like—are not commendable, and a person should change those attitudes and behaviors. Proverbs reinforces the admonition from Ephesians that if we are to change an undesirable behavioral pattern, that means that the trait by itself is changeable, rather than fixed.

The next and most important question became, How does a district officer assess whether the proclivity to become angry is under control? ("Under control" means few emotional outbursts or hostile acts that might intimidate or harm a person.) He does so by looking for the key temperament trait of Self-Discipline (one of the five primary traits in the MAX Report). This single temperament trait keeps a lid on most of a person's eccentric and socially unacceptable behaviors. Self-Discipline keeps our excesses under control. Look at the candidate's Self-Discipline test score. We have found this test score to be consistently reliable. If there's continuing doubt, the assessor can then apply interview validation questions and check references.

What about the Introvert and Extrovert traits? We draw attention to these as they can be misunderstood and can lead to unfair evaluation of a candidate. As with other temperament traits, behavioral patterns of these traits can change. The results of Dale Carnegie training demonstrate the truth of this. Also, one's self-esteem or lack of it can have a profound impact on the behavior resulting from these traits. Further, I (John) have not found any correlation between the Introvert trait and the natural talent of Singular Relational. Here's the difference. If a person appears to be Introverted, he can learn to be more sociable, and that learning process is not contradicting God's design in him. On the other hand, one who is gifted with the Singular Relational talent is to use this talent for the glory of God just as it is. But even that doesn't limit the person as much as you might think. For example, we find that among Singular Relationals there are warm Singulars and cold Singulars, thereby suggesting that some Singulars are more extroverted and some more introverted.

> *Trying to become a Multi Relational-talented person by attending a Dale Carnegie seminar would be disobeying God's design.*

Trying to become a Multi-Relational-talented person by attending a Dale Carnegie seminar would be disobeying God's design. We are encouraged to change our behavior (and our temperament traits, such as patience, kindness, and faith) to conform to the image of Christ. We are not to change our natural talents. Rather, recognizing them and using them allows us to conform to the image of Christ, the way God intended.

For example, some successful ministry leaders I (Don) know well have demonstrated that they have the Singular Relational talent. In some cases, they have assumed they are introverted and tried to change that orientation. It has been most helpful to share with them that the Singular talent is not a flaw or something to deny. We assure them that it is a strength that God has given, and we urge them not to operate under the burden that they should be different. Instead, they must craft their ministry around the strengths God gave them. They might:

- Choose senior staff and lay leaders who complement their relational talent and balance the team.

- Plan to stay for the long haul; a Singular Relational tends toward lifelong relationships.

- Work as a team with a spouse who makes friends more quickly in social settings where the Singular feels uncomfortable.

- Memorize a short list of questions they can ask any new acquaintance, and let others do most of the talking.

Internalizing these insights regarding the transformation of our temperament traits is an important step toward understanding what we are to change or improve regarding our personhood, and which traits God has put in us that do not need changing. This contributes to a leader's longevity in ministry—the topic of our next chapter.

Chapter 8
Nurturing Longevity

Moses' father-in-law replied, "What you are doing is not good. You and these people who come to you will only wear yourselves out. The work is too heavy for you; you cannot handle it alone." (Exodus 18:17-18)

Christian leaders candidly admit that they spend up to 80 percent of their time doing things at which they are second best. WHY? Unseized time will flow in the direction of one's relative weakness.
—*Gordon MacDonald,* Ordering Your Private World

I (John) recall a client bio that began in the middle, not at the beginning. A pastor contacted me saying that he felt somewhat constrained in his role and wanted to explore what he might do to improve his role as leader of his congregation. After completing an assessment of his strengths, I was surprised to discover that this thirty-something pastor had a talent strength in Speaking (preaching), was Multi-Relational, and had the Initiator/ Developer talent. This is one of the rarest combinations in one person. A readymade five-star church planter!

So why was he frustrated? I learned that he did not plant the church where he pastored, and the congregation, stuck in their traditions, was not willing to move forward to meet his capacity to lead to new levels. He was like a V8 trying to move an all-terrain vehicle. I understood the frustration completely. As we discussed his options for being a church planter or a ministry entrepreneur, he remarked that his family came from a country in the Baltic region of northern Europe. He had always had a soft spot for his family's homeland. I pointed out that if he had a vision to start a ministry there, he had all the natural talents to make it happen. And he did make it happen. Twenty years later the ministry is going strong. He's even received recognition and endorsements from the nation's president, who gave him public praise. What is more, the church he left fully supports him and provides multiple volunteers for short-term teams.

> **Had this man stayed in his existing pastoral role, he could easily have burned out and dropped out of ministry.**

If this man had stayed in his existing pastoral role, he could easily have burned out and dropped out of ministry. We know that far too many pastors who once felt called to vocational ministry have dropped out. Obtaining accurate statistics is tricky. Widely circulated figures that 80-90 percent of pastors will leave vocational ministry before they retire seem to be extrapolated from studies done by Fuller Seminary in the 1980s and 1990s. This alarming and possibly unreliable number was picked up and repeated by Focus on the Family[3] and later published by influencers such as John Ortberg in *Leadership Journal.*[4]

However, other studies, which assessed pastor attrition after ten years—such as one conducted by the Auburn Seminary Institute in 2008—give a different view. Their study found a 10-percent attrition rate after a decade among seminary graduates, and about twice that among strictly evangelical and independent church clergy.[5]

Whatever the actual dropout rate, it is too high. Some of that number "failed out." But not all. We know of gifted leaders with healthy marriages and godly character who today are working in the food industry, sales, or the trades. Nothing wrong with that work, but it was not their original calling. They would claim to have burned out emotionally from the pressure of pastoring. Perhaps some will reenter, but many of them have no intention to return.

We wish there was one common thread in their stories. The stated reasons for leaving full-time ministry widely vary. But it is remarkable to find many instances in which the wheels came off the wagon between ages thirty-five and forty-five, just at the threshold of the pastors' prime years. We believe that many of those departures are unnecessary, and that the body of Christ loses some much-needed ministry leaders.

So what can be done to extend one's ministry life and effectiveness now? How could someone thinking of reentering ministry approach it more wisely a second time? We find several key principles to longevity in pastoral ministry.

The 60/40 Principle

One of the most surprising principles that drew gasps from our district leaders during training was *the 60/40 principle.* In short the principle reads as follows:

The best you can realistically expect for your work is that 60 percent of your time will be spent on tasks that draw on your natural talent strengths.

This should be good news, but it can also be troubling. The good news is that no job in churches or elsewhere can possibly use 100 percent of a person's talent strengths all of the time. If there were, there would be very unhappy boards, managers, and presidents. Pastors and employees would be into entitlement: God hardwired me this way, therefore I should do things this way. The 60/40 principle acknowledges that while on earth, things are constantly changing. Finances, membership size, church staff, costs for operating the church building, and so on. In order to embrace those changes, senior management needs the flexibility of all personnel to make adjustments to keep the ship moving forward. So that means a pastor may have started with a job description, but two years later due to lower membership tithing, the associate pastor may have to go. Those job duties will have to be spread around among existing staff.

60/40 Principle

A fair balance is 60 percent of one's time using one's talent strengths. Actually, when discussing with clients who have accomplished this, they state that the joy of having a job that uses their strengths 60 percent of the time makes the other 40 percent not as frustrating. Yet their performance in the 40 percent will be less productive than in the 60 percent.

This brings up a second part of the principle. In essence, the paradigm advocates a double standard for job performance. We are to pursue excellence in the 60 percent and adequacy in the 40 percent. Managers who oversee subordinates will gain a much happier work crew when they implement the double standard, providing that all the team players are secure in their 60 percent. To expect the same level of output from one's 40-percent duties, which do not match one's talent strengths, only produces stress, which eventually will undermine the performance in one's strengths. We have the tendency to spend more time trying to shore up marginal performance, robbing the time from maximizing our strengths. For example, a gifted preacher might shortcut sermon preparation time to work on budgets, visitation, office admin, and the like.

> *We are to pursue excellence in the 60 percent and adequacy in the 40 percent.*

The third and last portion of the 60/40 principle focuses on the number of talent strengths that a person can expect to use in their sweet spot, the 60 percent. Since each person has between five and nine natural talent strengths, only three or four can be expected to be central for a job. So this means that up to half of a person's gifting is not being utilized at work. This is the norm; to seek a job that uses more talents is futile, and if even found, in a short time this will change.

Those leftover talents need to find an outlet, such as parenting duties, volunteer activities, hobbies, church activities, and the like. The key is to balance these extracurricular activities between opportunities to use your talent strengths and "urgent" needs that draw you out of your talent strengths. Gardening is not my (John's) thing, but I am the digger, weed puller, rototiller, greenhouse builder, and overall gofer for my wife, and I have also volunteered several times to do the local school beautification community service project with our church. Yet these do not define my identity; my junior high sail-boating instruction, cowboy western guitar playing, and home construction projects are my joy.

The Age Thirty Principle

When I (John) saw a frown come over the district officer sitting to my right, I sensed that something was troubling him. It usually happens at least once in each training seminar. Eventually, his hand went up.

"I guess I don't understand something," he said. "When I was starting in my pastorate, I had to do most everything, whether I was good at it or not. And overall, I did a good job. If I am hearing you right, I will be good at the job duties only when I am using my talent strengths. Well, my test results show that I am Singular Relational, but even if I am, I still had to meet and greet my congregation regardless. So I'm having a hard time accepting that one can't change his talents based on the needs of the job."

I was so thankful for my previous nineteen years of study, research, and trial and error that preceded the training Don and I were doing. These trainees were seasoned men, selected by their peers to be district leaders, the cream of the crop. Perhaps you have had that same question. The answer over time has come to be known as the *age thirty principle*.

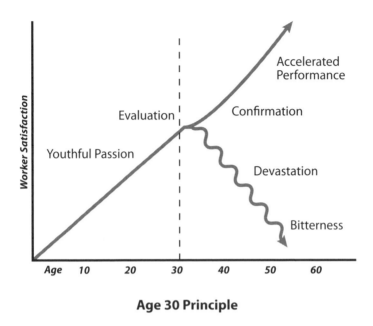

Age 30 Principle

The principle tries to explain how a person can perform well outside of their talent strengths for a sustained period of time in their early years of ministry. However, if by age thirty to thirty-five, a person's core duties do not align with their talent strengths, there will be a decline of performance compounded by severe stress, perhaps depression, medical issues, need for extended time away, and the like. The key is what happens to our bodies at about age thirty.

Up until we are thirty, we have multiple opportunities to be exposed to different types of activities. At school we have art, music, sports, auto shop, home economics, chemistry, creative writing, speech class, student government, exchange students, short-term mission trips, and on and on. Not only does each of these activities bring a sense of fulfillment or dissatisfaction, but there is usually someone watching—parents, grandparents, teachers, youth pastors, and peers—and cheering you on, adding external incentive. Now, if you played the clarinet and it was ho hum to you, but you received a standing ovation and your circle of adults continued to praise you and ask for more, guess what? You would probably continue on that track. People would begin to call you a clarinet player, and you would hang out with the band or orchestra kids. Praise from our esteemed community carries a lot of weight in motivating us to do certain activities.

Now you are choosing to go to college. Mom and Dad are still on the clarinet cheering squad, so guess what? You select music as your major, and in order to make a living, you decide to be a music teacher. At this point you don't care how God has gifted you; things are working fine. You accept the first teaching job offered and become the music teacher for Central Junior High. Good school, good pay, you are set. For the first few years things seem to be going great. There are good parts to the job, and parts that are stressful. *But isn't every job like that?* you reason.

> *One who is gifted learns to improve by intuitive trial and error.*

A new opportunity comes along to teach at a high school. You take the job, thinking that this is a much better opportunity to move ahead. By now you are about twenty-eight, and you decide it is time to marry your girlfriend of the last two years. She is a middle school teacher and loves her job. Two years into the marriage you have a new child. On the job front you find that the stress from your work is increasing. You feel as though you go home exhausted and then return to campus exhausted. You have little energy to embrace your family's needs for your involvement. Your wife is carrying more of the family management ball.

Okay, let's stop the narrative at this moment. Several important things have happened without your notice. First, your emotional rubber band is stretched so far that you have little reserve to give your family and students. This stretch is coming from three sources. Your marriage is new. You have a baby to care for, and that takes up energy. And last, your body has passed that critical divide at age thirty. Sometime during that year, your trillions of body cells, which have been birthing and dying, change their ratio. Before thirty the birthing rate of cells is faster than the dying rate. This means that you can engage in stressful job duties and have that stress healed by a good night's sleep and a couple days of weekend time off because new body cells are replacing the dying stress cells faster than they are dying off. But at age thirty, the rate of birthing begins to slow down, so that eventually the dying rate exceeds the birthing rate. So after thirty it takes more than a good night's sleep and a couple of weekend days to replenish the dying stress cells. There aren't any new cells to provide that renewal that you have gotten used to for the past ten years. Your coping mechanism isn't working as it used to. Now, this is a gradual process, but it is real.

Let's return to the district leader who asked the question about his earlier pastor days when he had to be a jack of all trades to do the job. Here we find the answer to why he was able to do so many things that were outside of his talent mix and bring forth an acceptable performance. As long as he was self-disciplined and focused, he could pull it off. As soon as he got married and then had a child, his ability to cope with the job stress grew less, as these home activities began using up a lot of energy that he used to give to the job. And finally, around age thirty his body changed and was no longer able to renew itself from the stress as readily. That's why a person can appear to be good at doing something but not be living from their talent strength core.

Now, there is something more to this principle. Let's look at a different life—say someone who did understand his strengths and chose to align the core of his job (the 60 percent) with his strengths. He has the same lumps and bumps as the rest of us, but there is also a surge of joy coming from using his strengths.

Every year he gets better and better. It's in the nature of the talents. One who is gifted learns to improve by intuitive trial and error. Another person, who is not gifted, will only grow by attending a seminar, reading a book, or inviting a more seasoned person to train him. He lacks the intuitive insights to "figure it out" for himself.

Think about what that process of trial and error leads to down the road for the gifted person. In addition to exemplary performance, eventually it leads to mastery. Something in earlier years might take a few hours, and now it takes a few minutes. I recall a true-life example from Albert Einstein. When working on a consulting project, he was able to assist a manufacturing firm in resolving a major technical issue. It took him a few minutes after going to the plant location to identify the problem. When he sent his invoice, he received a scathing rebuke. How could he charge the firm $10,000 for his services when he spent only a few minutes at the plant? Einstein wisely responded, "For my time to figure out the one problem at your plant, I charged you one hundred dollars. For my past twenty years of trial and error to eliminate all the other possible solutions, $9,900."

So at about age fifty-five or so, if we have been applying our talent strengths to 60 percent of our job, we begin to approach what I call *mastery*. This means that older workers are much more valuable to their churches than younger, more energetic workers. A seasoned pastor who knows and uses his strengths is far more effective than a pastor in his first ten years of ministry. Proverbs 22:29 says it well: "Do you see a man skilled in his work? He will serve before kings." I also suspect that Bezalel and Oholiab—the foremen for the tabernacle construction project—were not only gifted by God as Exodus 31:6 says, but they most likely were also seasoned craftsmen, respected by their peers.

Church Matching 201

Trying to fit the right pastor in the right church has been an ongoing learning process, and we've made progress. This is good news for pastors' longevity on the job, because the right church match can mean the difference between thriving and dying.

In the Alliance, each pastor referral to a church must be prescreened by the district office. Using the talent profiles as a guide, a district officer is now able to more accurately refer candidates to the best matches from among the multitude of churches in his state. Following are a few of the placement principles that have been discovered over time.

If a church is experiencing some type of conflict, two talents become important in the pastor. The first is the Problem Solving talent. With this strength, the pastor candidate is able to discern the root issues that are causing the conflict and address them. The second talent requires some relational strengths to win the trust and respect of congregation members quickly, thus the Familiar Group talent or maybe the Multi-Relational talent. However the Singular Relational talent does not fit this situation.

If a church was one hundred or fewer people, the Multi-Relational talent might seem to be the desired trait to bring in new members. Yet, to the contrary, while we've found that the Multi talent is very effective in winning most everyone's trust and respect in six months, it then starts bringing in strangers and treats them like founding fathers, causing resentment among established members. Multi-Relationals should not be referred to small churches, even if the churches want to grow. Multi-Relationals should be placed with medium (three-hundred-plus) and large churches (one-thousand-plus).

If a church appears to be more traditional and resistant to change or innovation, a pastor candidate with Order of Space talent is a much better fit than a Creative-talented pastor.

The Creative pastor would want to continually change things, thereby causing conflict.

Multi-Relationals should not be referred to small churches, even if the churches want to grow.

If a church has a tradition of a shepherding pastor—one who was strong on visitation, caring for the sick and bereaved—a candidate with one of the Helping or Nurturing talents would fit best. The opposite, the Initiating/Developing, talent would be disaster. I recall one situation where a non-Alliance denomination referred a pastor to my office. That district stated that the church had multiple complaints about the pastor, who had been on the job less than two years. They asked me to complete a full assessment to try to unravel what the core of the conflict was about. During the meetings with the pastor, I learned that he had sensed a calling to the pastorate, sold his successful business, attended seminary, and was placed in that church by that denomination's office. The talent profile that unfolded for him was that of an Initiator/Developer. Sadly, the office had not considered how his entrepreneurial talent would impact a small traditional church, which was used to a shepherding type of pastor. When I revealed the results of the assessment, I sought to point out that the pastor was very gifted and should be quickly reassigned to a better church fit. I also recommended that the next pastor sent to the traditional church should have a more shepherding approach to ministry. Hopefully both the pastor and the church were saved from disaster.

If a church represents a more agrarian congregation or perhaps a large number of blue collar or trades members, then a pastor with an Analyzing or Problem Solving talent might not be a good fit. These talents cause the person to tend to like to be somewhat scholarly, using the Greek and Hebrew.

If a church is seeking to emphasize evangelistic outreach, the best talent would be a Multi-Relational pastor—the Promoting talent is also helpful—who most naturally is inclined to befriend strangers and lead others to do the same. On the other hand, if a church seeks to focus on member discipleship, the Familiar Group talent is optimum due to that person's emphasis on maintaining and deepening relationships over many years.

Of Coaches and Ladders

Judge   Coach

Leadership Style

When we started our training, the typical district leader doing assessment conducted himself with the traditional countenance of a judge, frowning at the candidate, lording the assessment process over him. We were successful in promoting an alternative countenance—that of a coach, one who tries to understand a candidate's strengths in order to direct him into a successful, lifelong ministry. In order to be a coach, the interviewer needs to have a large bucket of alternative ministry leadership options available. Each candidate applying for a pastor position tends to make a strong statement that he is seeking a leadership role.

After all, the apostle Paul said that the desire to be a ministry leader is a noble thing (1 Timothy 3:1). If the only role available is senior pastor, then the interviewer is doomed to be a gate keeper, permitting only a very few to enter. However, if that interviewer has 20,000 ministry leadership options, then the outcome is a win-win for all.

To train the district leaders to a coaching style of assessment, we had to redefine the role of a leader. We succeeded in identifying two types of leaders, calling the ascension to each "climbing the leadership ladder."

Specialist   Supervisor

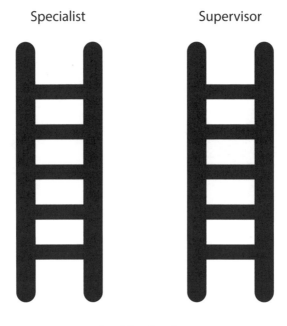

Ladder Analogy

The first ladder, labeled Specialist, fits most leadership aspirants. It acknowledges a candidate who correctly identifies his strengths and then finds the appropriate position—not necessarily that of a pastor. Over time, this individual achieves mastery in his or her specialty and becomes a leader (though seldom in name) who attracts a following. One does not have to look far to find these leaders, who are most everywhere: excellent teachers, gifted counselors, exceptional youth workers, and the like. One can also include church members who excel in the performance of their jobs and thereby gain the admiration of their peers, leading to roles such as deacon or elder.

The second ladder, open to fewer leaders, is labeled Supervisor. On this ladder are those who are in charge of others. These individuals, because of the responsibility of their position, require closer scrutiny. It is on this second ladder that we find the single-cell pastor and the multiple-cell pastor.

Recognizing the two ladders has significantly helped district leaders direct young aspiring men to a future that has allowed them to become the best kinds of leaders that God made them to be.

We now change our emphasis from insights gained over twenty-five years to those issues and beliefs that we've found separate those who effectively apply the assessment process from those who don't.

PART IV

The Great Divides

Chapter **9**

Watershed Issues for District Supervisors and Educators

"Neither is new wine put into old wineskins. If it is, the skins burst and the wine is spilled and the skins are destroyed. But new wine is put into fresh wineskins, and so both are preserved." (Matthew 9:17, ESV)

It is the test of an organization to make ordinary human beings perform better than they seem capable of, to bring out whatever strength there is in its members.
—Peter Drucker, Management

When most people think about the Continental Divide, they picture the jagged, rocky line running the length of the Rocky Mountains that separates the drainage of snow melt to the west or to the east. In my (Don's) state of Minnesota, the much-less-famous Laurentian Divide stretches across the northern reaches. I've crossed it many times in the town of Brown Valley. All the visitor sees is an almost-imperceptible rise running east and west. How significant could that be? Yet it's enough to form an incredible divide. A drop of rain or flake of snow falling on the north side drains into the Red River, flows north through Fargo and Winnipeg, into Lake Winnipeg, and eventually to the Hudson Bay. Whereas a drop of moisture landing south of the divide flows into the Minnesota and Mississippi river basins and ends up in the Gulf of Mexico. Two raindrops falling only a foot apart can end up in extremely different climes.

Figuratively speaking, our work in pastoral assessment has clarified a multifaceted divide for our district leadership. Though barely perceptible at first, it became more apparent as we went along. I distinctly remember when one of our superintendents reached a watershed moment. Partway through his training, he broke in to remark: "If I start working with people this way, it will entirely change my job!" He merely gave voice to what others were feeling. After they were trained in a new assessment paradigm, things would never be the same again.

Chapters 9 and 10 explain several related watershed issues for your consideration.

- Chapter 9 focuses on issues of special interest to *district supervisors and educators*—those responsible for preparation and placement of pastoral candidates.

- Chapter 10 presents issues of interest to *pastors*, and we welcome pastors to skip ahead and read chapter 10.

Your choice of "east" or "west" on each of these issues will make the difference between, on the one hand, appreciating and benefiting fully from this assessment process and, on the other hand, misunderstanding and missing out on the full benefit.

Stewarding God's Greatest Resource

Fundamentally, doing proper assessment is Christian stewardship. How so? Stewards are not owners. They take care of the possessions of another. Christian stewardship is defined simply as the use of divinely entrusted resources for the purposes intended by God (Psalm 24:1; Matthew 25:14-30; 1 Corinthians 4:1-2; 6:19-20; 10:26; and more).

What is the greatest resource of the church of Jesus Christ on earth? Is it money, or buildings, or technology, or educational institutions? I submit that greater than all of those are the people!

Fundamentally, doing good assessment is Christian stewardship.

Those people God calls and equips for ministry leadership are a precious resource He provides to His body. One need look no further than Ephesians 4 to see just how valuable. The text says it is the ascended Christ Himself who gave gifts— apostles, prophets, evangelists, and pastors and teachers—to the church (4:11). If these *people* are the gifts—probably the best interpretation of the verse—then think of the implication. Their origin, their appointment, their very ministry is defined by Jesus. They do not appoint themselves to the church, they are *given* to the church—for the express purpose of equipping the saints for the work of ministry (4:12).

Thus, with that resource comes responsibility. Responsibility on the part of the person who has received God's calling. And on the part of the persons who place those individuals within the body.

Thus it is wise and good stewardship before the Lord to make placement recommendations in light of how He has hardwired each individual who seeks the pastorate. A wise placement decision is made with knowledge of the fit between the individual and a particular ministry. That is stewarding the person properly, as God intended.

However, if placements are made without such knowledge, or the implications are ignored, the results are damaging across the board, if not catastrophic. That is poor stewardship.

Integrally related is the financial support of church-planting projects. We've hardly mentioned that aspect, deliberately.

If the primary stewardship is done well, so that people who are innately talented for the startup of a church are identified, then money is secondary.

One temptation we found among our leaders was to make the money available for a church plant in the budget, and then to go out and find someone willing to attempt the startup. That puts the cart before the horse! The project will be more likely to succeed if the right person is chosen up front to lead it.

The dollars must flow to the project after the planter selection has been made and affirmed. We thus assure good stewardship of both people and treasure, in that order.

The good news is that our leaders across the U.S. take their stewardship seriously. They eagerly desire to know how to assess pastoral candidates wisely. And armed with that knowledge, they help more people enter ministries where they fit well and the impact is positive. When this practice began, the casualty rate dropped dramatically as a result. And, consequently, the investment of precious dollars produces a harvest.

The Role of Spiritual Gifts

One of the points of confusion in assessment is the place of spiritual gifts in relation to innate aptitudes.

Popular Christian teaching on ministry strengths focuses on the spiritual gifts, whether, for example, it's the venerable Wagner-Houts Spiritual Gifts Inventory or the more recent eighty-question APEST (apostle, prophet, evangelist, pastor, teacher) Revised Fivefold Ministries Inventory. The typical methodology is to base the presence of gifts on self-reported patterns of behavior in relationships and ministry, along with what peers and advisors name as the person's strengths.

We know that what follows may counter some popular thinking on the subject, but consider with us three observations.

First, this emphasis on gifts alone is lopsided. It focuses almost entirely on the spiritual factor, while discounting or overlooking the aptitude factor underlying what maximizes the service of a ministry leader.

Second, we are uncomfortable defining spiritual gifts so heavily in behavioral terms—good listening, liking to teach, and so on. This seems to understate what should be the defining mark of a spiritual gift—*supernatural* effects. Spiritual fruit and edification are more to the point than personally preferred behaviors.

That leads to the third and most significant observation. Behavioral indicators often point to the presence of innate aptitudes or talents. We argue that some of the popular inventories are in reality uncovering and measuring the presence of talent strengths even more than the spiritual gifts! The two categories should not be confused. To do so introduces an unnecessary blur into the portrait that assessment seeks to discover.

To be sure, our point is not to dismiss such inventories—just to assert two key points: that spiritual gifts and innate talents are two separate "equippings" by God, and that to be complete, assessment must include identification of innate talents. This part of the person is far too important to leave out.

Spiritual gifts and innate talents are two separate "equippings" by God.

Here is what we have learned about how spiritual gifts and innate talents interact:

- Both spiritual gifts and natural talents come from the same source—our Creator God. They are valuable trusts from Him.

- However, spiritual gifts and natural talents differ in several ways:

- All persons seem to be endowed with certain innate talent strengths.

- Only members of Christ's body receive spiritual gifts, as the Holy Spirit determines (1 Corinthians 12:7,11).

- An innate talent may have a powerful effect in the natural human realm. While a spiritual gift empowers supernatural effects and capacity.

• There is no one-to-one correlation between vocation and spiritual gifts. One who teaches school well does not necessarily have the spiritual gift of teaching, nor does the business owner always have the gift of administration.

• Spiritual gifts and innate aptitudes *may be* related in ministry practice. Suppose a person with an innate talent for communicating through vocal music also has the spiritual gift of mercy. Singing is not the spiritual gift. And the mercy gift is not the singing. However, the Holy Spirit may use both to minister divine comfort in the hearts of the audience, using the singer's vocal performance and interpretation of the lyrics.

• Though the functioning of spiritual gifts is a uniquely Christian experience, assessment without accounting for the role of natural talents is a weak indicator of competent and effective ministry in a particular role.

• The list of traits required by Paul for church leaders does not include spiritual gifts (1 Timothy 3; Titus 1).

• We highly recommend the implementation of a natural talents assessment, like that of IDAK, in addition to a spiritual gifts assessment.

Finally, we must acknowledge that Christians have no corner on understanding the powerful potential of natural talents. It doesn't require a specific religious belief or perspective to observe aptitude strengths at work and to identify them. Lots of HR professionals, career coaches, trainers, and business gurus have figured out the connection between inborn talent and work performance. But unique to *Christian* assessment is the recognition of both innate talents *and* the spiritual gifts as God's equipping for ministry.

This is a watershed issue for those who prepare and oversee Christian ministry leaders. Why? They can build into their work a strong and fuller assessment of their candidates and development for their current personnel. We believe a process that takes innate abilities into account strengthens the basis for wise decisions and honors God, the true source of gifts and talents. The alternative is to overlook the talent factor and miss wisdom that God may wish to impart. One of the main purposes of this book is to empower all leaders—those who want to develop their capacity for better recruitment, training, and placement.

Innate or Learned?

This question concerning key pastoral skills was of huge importance and led us to make a major paradigm shift. The traditional model of pastoral education assumes that students can be trained to do all the different ministries the body of Christ needs. Skill acquisition through study, hard work, field experience, and repetition is the path. At times this approach borders on the ridiculous. One prominent evangelical seminary cites on its website five competency areas for students to develop: leadership, pastoral care, personal and spiritual development, proclamation, and relational skills. Well enough. However, listed under each area are specific skills that the minister should master—a total of *seventy-three* to be exact! How could any one person in a single lifetime ever meet the standard?

No wonder that, once out in ministry, Christian workers flock to pastoral seminars where gifted leaders offer them skill training. Some of the biggest names claim that attendees can become great leaders also, if they will learn and apply the skills taught by the expert. I (Don) attended more than my share of these over the years, in the belief that I could learn just about any ministerial leadership skill through hard work.

In the secular world, a similar assumption has been widely accepted. One of its most recent forms is the "10,000-hour rule," popularized by Malcolm Gladwell in his book *Outliers: The Story of Success*. The theory arose from a university study twenty years ago of budding German violinists over a decade, the most notable of which practiced intensely for an average of 10,000 hours and rose to elite performance. Dedicated practice yielded exceptional skill, so the theory went.[6]

If it is true that a skill can be developed by hours of intense practice, then the importance of innate talents in ministry assessment is much lower than we thought. That would imply that pastors and other church-related workers should be encouraged to follow the learned-skill paradigm: Identify the needed skills of the job and pursue mastery of them with rigorous study, practice, and discipline.

Recently, however, a scholarly meta-review of eighty-eight scientific studies concluded that while intense repetitive practice increases performance in brain games like chess as much as 26 percent, and music performance up to 18 percent, it increased sports performance only 4 percent, and produced a mere 1-percent gain in the professions.[7]

Devoting even incredibly long hours to skill development evidently has limitations. The paradigm shift for Alliance leaders was to grasp the incredible power of innate talent strengths as indicators of and motivators for ministry excellence.

Talents are those intuitive capacities within us. IDAK identifies them in three arenas: Communicational talents, Relational talents, and Functional (task-oriented) talents. Innate talents motivate a person to grow, develop, and make improvements eagerly and lifelong. They function almost effortlessly and energize the person, rather than draining energy. They grow by intuitive trial and error, continually evolving to higher levels of job mastery. A frequent illustration John uses is the growth of a tree. A natural tree will grow with the right amount of sun, nutrients, and water. The trunk and branches grow so that they are continually adequate to support the fruit. On the other hand, a plastic tree can grow only by gluing on branches and fruit. Eventually it will topple from the weight, because the plastic trunk cannot grow to meet the demand. The plastic tree is like a person trying to live outside of his or her innate talent core, futilely manu-facturing results rather than growing fruit naturally by use of one's natural talents.

Devoting even incredibly long hours to skill development evidently has limitations.

In contrast to innate talents, learned skills are capacities acquired through rote memory and repetitive effort, and are often limited to a specific task or job. The studies noted earlier showed that repetitive skill development yields only modest improvements in most endeavors. Had I (Don) known this distinction early in my ministry it would have saved me much frustration and even some guilt.

I was taught by the eminent Dr. Gary Collins at one of America's finest seminaries the skills to do pastoral counseling—how to set up the office to make people feel at ease, showing empathy, listening intently, choosing the right responses from the pastor's repertoire, and bringing Scripture to bear on the issues. The instruction was high-quality and it still makes me grateful.

After graduation, some of my new ministry peers talked excitedly about how they loved listening to a troubled member or a needy couple. They spoke of no limits to their patience; they were willing to meet whenever that person wanted to come back and talk. But that was not my experience. Within a few minutes listening to a counselee, I'd jump ahead, thinking, *Here's the real problem*—even as the narrative continued. I would then offer solutions, describe actions to bring about healthy changes, naively expecting that would take care of the problem. But that rarely happened. Most people returned, only to cover the same ground each time. Inside I squirmed.

Because I had learned some counseling skills, I forced myself to endure these repetitive sessions while blaming myself for impatience. To remedy this, I participated in pastoral counseling seminars and read more books on the subject. While the mechanics of my counseling improved, my fundamental frustration did not go away.

Years later, through my own personal IDAK assessment, I learned why. First, I did not have the Helping talent of counseling. Second, I do have the Problem-Solving talent. It comes naturally to me. That's why I would jump ahead to formulate solutions to the counselee's problem, shortcutting the empathy and the time that intense listening takes.

By sheer dint of effort I made myself improve my skills. But they never came easily or naturally. I seriously doubt now that 10,000 hours of practice would have made me an expert in that arena; rather, it would have brought on burnout!

This personal experience (told in hopes that my counselor friends will show grace) highlights for me what today is an obvious distinction between the operation of learned skills versus innate talents.

The beautiful thing is that no pastor—no one in the body of Christ—has every talent or all the spiritual gifts. There may well be others in local churches with the needed talent who would thrive by being someone's first-line counselor. And there are truly gifted professionals to call on when more help is called for.

This distinction is among the most important watershed issues for a ministry leader to get right. Our observation is that many well-meaning servants of Christ take on positions that are simply not a fit, based on their innate talent profile. They strive and struggle to carry out the required actions for that position, sometimes with incredible devotion. But after the novelty wears off, or they reach middle age, they end up frustrated, drained, and often blaming themselves for underperformance.

One common reason is that the majority of their duties require skills that do not come naturally, and not nearly enough time is left for the ministries they do well and enjoy. This poor fit is a sure formula for feeling drained and stressed. We cannot prove it, but it seems likely that part of the ministry burnout phenomenon is really the stress of being in the wrong role or not realigning it with one's talents.

Thankfully, our assessment process helps more and more leaders identify where to focus their energies and strengths, as well as the aspects of ministry to delegate to volunteers or staff. When a leader is in the right role, ministering the majority of the time on the basis of God-given talents, he or she will be energized.

> *Part of the ministry burnout phenomenon is really the stress of being in the wrong role or not realigning it with one's talents.*

Women Gifted with the Church-Planting Talent

Talents have not been found to be gender restricted. Our experience confirms that all of the talents are present in both men and women. That is true when assessing for the church-planting talent. A woman, whether she is single or married, may have been gifted by God to be a starter, an initiator. Such a talent can and should be affirmed.

It is the church's role, however, to exegete Scripture. Some would understand that a woman could be the lead person in a startup church. Others, our fellowship included, understand the passages on eldership in the New Testament to show that a woman would not take on that authority herself. But certainly that does not preclude her from being a major partner in a startup team or from launching and leading significant ministries within a new church.

Wherever one comes out on scriptural teaching, it is vital that an assessment and placement process make room in the church for both men and women with the Initiating/Developing talent.

Norming Psychological Tests

In addition to natural talents, temperament or personality traits are important for placement decisions. Traits such as Character, Self-Esteem, Self-Discipline, and Team Player are vital in determining qualified candidates. In an earlier chapter we described the way that we re-normed existing temperament/ personality (psychological) tests to match the ideal profiles for established pastors and for church planters. This provides an accurate target for comparison of a candidate's psych profile with that of successful practitioners in the field. We know from experience that making placements based on the original, unadapted test profiles is a less reliable way of guiding candidates than using the re-normed profiles. This is a significant watershed decision for those responsible for candidate guidance and placement. We strongly encourage assessors to use the adapted test norms for the 16PF and TJTA instruments developed by IDAK.

Bigger Church Size, Same Talents?

Early during our training of district officers, we began to notice a prevailing assumption that if a pastor was successful with three hundred, he could grow that church to three thousand. The erroneous assumption was that the pastor only needed the appropriate training in order to make the transition. District officers who believed this assumption failed to grasp the importance of the single- and multiple-cell principle of church leadership. This principle goes a long way to explain why the far majority of U.S. churches are approximately one hundred members in size.

A single-cell pastor leads effectively when all his subordinates are doing tasks that are integrated and where the pastor is the most knowledgeable source for most everything that goes on. It is like a basketball team coach or a baseball team coach. One person is the expert. All the members look up to the single coach. If you don't know, ask Pastor Sam. This model works for up to 350 members. If a church continues to grow, it requires a leader who can coordinate the expanding ministries that are not in his experience bag. A new set of talents is needed, meaning a new pastor. An executive pastor with one of the talents is a very acceptable substitute, allowing the original pastor to continue.

As Jethro counseled Moses, the number of Israelites was far too great for him to continue as the solo resource. But in pastoring, the solution is not as simple as Jethro's advice—just find competent others and you decide the important cases. Actually, Jethro's model is a single-cell approach, as Moses was the most knowledgeable of the judges and was able to continue exercising the same talents.

I (John) recall an unusual situation that came to me from the Midwest. A growing independent Bible church with a dynamic radio ministry was considering raising funds to build a substantially larger church complex. The board chairman was concerned that perhaps the financial commitment of millions of dollars to build might exceed the pastor's leadership ability to manage. We agreed to complete an assessment on the pastor. I was delighted to report to the chairman and the elders that indeed the pastor had such a talent that equipped him to oversee multiple teams—the Initiating/Developing talent, the very same talent needed for church planters. Twenty years later the same pastor is still at the church, which continues to grow and thrive.

A multiple-cell church pastor is gifted with a Supervisory talent (Initiating/Developing and Managing; occasionally the Long-Range Planning talent can qualify) so that he can coordinate the work of many subordinates who are doing independent and unrelated ministries. His role is to continually bring cooperation and harmony among the other leaders, each wanting his or her ministry to gain the priority attention, budget, classroom space, calendar dates, and pulpit promotion. An appropriate illustration of the multiple-cell church is to compare it to the athletic department of a high school. The athletic director supervises all of the coaches, each representing a different sport. To ensure cooperation and harmony among the coaches, one needs a Supervisory talent.

Before departing this topic of multiple-cell pastors, I recall another unusual assessment project. I (John) was contacted by a church-plant pastor in Las Vegas who had a well-established church. This church was growing because it was ministering to drug addicts, alcoholics, and prostitutes, rather than attracting members from other churches. Yet the lead pastor began to acknowledge he might have a problem in how he was managing his pastoral staff. They were threatening to walk out on him. This was not the first or second, but the third time this happened. After completing an assessment, I recognized that he had the Initiating/Developing talent, which had empowered him not only to plant the church, but to continue growing it, including a K-12 school and the planting of five daughter churches within ten miles of the parent church. His style of management was characterized as rough, insensitive, uncaring. The threatened walkout was because he did not listen to and care for his staff, as would a shepherd. I explained to him that he was managing his staff as if they were gifted as he was—take the bull by the horns, charge up the hill. Further, he needed to continue to have new horizons to conquer if he was to stay at that church. Wisely his elders allowed him considerable latitude for growth. This insight led him to complete a pastoral audit of his five key pastors and to add a new executive pastor with a Planning talent. Peace was restored. I kept in touch over the next ten years and was delighted to hear how the church continued to minister to the community. I also learned that he was very active in planting churches in the Philippines and was teaching church planting for his denomination.

Is "Calling" Enough?

One of the most frequent questions asked of candidates is, "Describe your calling to ministry service." So young seminarians are taught to be sure that they can describe this prompting of God in very clear and persuasive terms so as to convince a licensing and ordination council that something supernatural happened and that they should be licensed. District officers who depended merely on description of an authentic call, without seeking evidence of community confirmation and the suitable God-given talents, were not strong users of our assessment process.

That isn't to say that qualified pastor candidates were not placed, but there would always be a mystery for the next district officer to unravel when that pastor experienced his first congregational complaint—no verifiable evidence of the pastor's aptitude strengths.

The Rare Church-Planter Talent

As long as a district officer believed that many of the church-planter traits could be learned from a boot-camp training experience, there was less buy-in to the assessment process— particularly to the need for the key Initiator/Developer talent.

Sadly, youth with this talent are not the favorite of the youth pastor. These young men are pushing the boundaries of authority, they do not toe the party line. They may challenge most everything just for the thrill of it. So few are eager to look beyond the wild behavior to assess whether there is an Initiating/Developing talent. It requires a savvy youth pastor who is not easily intimidated and has a healthy self-esteem.

Whether or not a district leader recognizes the sparseness of the Initiating/Developing talent is a watershed issue. Those who don't will continue placing ill-suited candidates in poorly matched leadership roles. Those who do are much more likely to make the best placements and will be more willing to cast the wider net to actively recruit this rare talent.

Passively Wait or Actively Recruit?

Given the socially challenging behavior of a young Initiator/Developer, it is no surprise that district officers or educators are not attracted to this type of person and therefore will not feel comfortable using assessment and recruitment efforts to lasso them in. The end result is, district leaders end up looking for church planters among the tame, obedient, and stable candidates. The saying, "It takes one to know one," couldn't be more appropriate. A seasoned church planter will recall his pushing-the-envelope youth and be able to motivate younger versions of himself with stories of his past. When I talk with leaders who have the Initiating/Developing talent, their story tends to be a common one: the youth pastor who, when young, starts out like a bull in a china closet. Eventually, he clashes with established leadership, who drive the youth pastor out. Some survive to become pastors at a more flexible church. Others leave full-time ministry entirely.

We need to be actively looking for these important young people among our college students and even our high schoolers.

They need our guidance and patience in order to become the church planters and spiritual entrepreneurs God intends them to be.

Cultural Sensitivity in Assessment

Knowing how to assess Western American young men is challenging enough, but multicultural candidates is another story altogether. District officers who assumed one size fits all were reluctant to adopt different assessment systems for their first- and second-generation pastor candidates. Since close to 45 percent of Alliance churches are non-Anglo, the need to be more culturally sensitive has become a watershed issue. Districts who do not use culturally sensitive assessment tools for their candidates of Vietnamese, Spanish, Hmong, Cambodian, and South Korean ancestry will fail at screening for pastors who can succeed within their own culture.

A key example for which cultural sensitivity is critical is the talent of Time and Priorities. The Asian, American, and European cultures highly prize this talent and build time efficiency into their job descriptions. However, the African and Latin American cultures do not value this talent as highly. Individuals in those cultures with that talent are taught to subordinate that trait so as to focus on more culturally important behaviors, such as developing genuine relationships, which take indeterminate amounts of time and cannot be structured by a clock. These cultural misfits who have the Time and Priorities talent become much more receptive to Western ideas and systems. But multicultural congregations may be more receptive to leaders with a different set of innate talents better suited to the specific culture.

The advances in developing multicultural assessment systems in the language of the culture have been significant. Both interviewing and online assessment instruments have been developed for each culture in its language. Each district superintendent must be trained to assess his leaders using their language. An important distinction is also made between first- and second-generation multicultural leaders, so that all districts can assess and honor second-generation candidates using their own cultural distinctives.

Interdistrict Trust

The need for trust of one district's assessment results by another district surfaced early in the process. If a district officer was more independent, not inclined to accept advice from others, it would follow that this person would want his own independent assessment process and would not assume the results of another district regarding a particular candidate. But this is an unnecessary waste of duplicated effort.

Some success in overcoming this roadblock was achieved with the requirement of each district to have one officer certified in the assessment process. This meant that the officer not only had been trained and had experience, but that he had submitted an audio recording and written report for examination. If acceptable, he was certified. Unfortunately, several district officers who thought they knew the process were not certified. In the end this certification process protected the denomination from inaccurate assessment results. However, the training and certification are still voluntary on the part of the district offices, and several districts have not complied with the appeal to work together for the good of the national movement.

Having shared these watershed issues for district officers, we next address watershed issues that seem to help or hinder pastors. District officers and educators may skip ahead to chapter 11.

Chapter **10**
Watershed Issues for Pastors

Woe to him who quarrels with his Maker. ...
Does the clay say to the potter,
*   "What are you making?" (Isaiah 45:9)*

Deep in our hearts, we all want to find and fulfill a purpose
bigger than ourselves. For each of us, the real purpose is
personal and passionate; to know what we are here to do,
and why.
—Os Guinness, The Call

If you are a pastor who has skipped over chapter 9, please read the first two paragraphs of chapter 9 about watersheds, real and figurative, and then come back and continue reading here.

Chapters 9 and 10 explain several related watershed issues for your consideration.

- Chapter 9 focuses on issues of special interest to *district supervisors and educators*—those responsible for preparation and placement of pastoral candidates. If you play such a role and have already read chapter 9, we welcome you to skip ahead and to continue reading at chapter 11.

- Chapter 10 presents issues of interest to *pastors*—watershed issues that are makers or breakers of the assessment process for those working on the "front lines" of church ministry.

Your choice of "east" or "west" on each of these issues will make the difference between, on the one hand, appreciating and benefiting fully from this assessment process and, on the other hand, misunderstanding and missing out on the full benefit.

Placing Your Talents on the Altar

Some pastors we've observed have been willing, as an act of obedience to the Lord, to place their talents on the altar and to seek to be the leaders God has formed them to be. Some have not been willing to submit to God's design for them. (There are many ways to excel as a leader, each calling for a different God-given talent or combination of talents. The obedience question is not whether or not to be a leader, but which leadership role best fits one's talents.) We've found that those who are willing to seek fresh guidance through self-assessment, even though it may lead in unfamiliar directions, have come away enthusiastic about their new knowledge concerning talents and how to uniquely maximize their ministry efforts.

We cannot emphasize this enough. Trying to learn how to do church the way a superstar does it will not work.

We cannot emphasize this enough. Trying to learn how to do church the way a superstar does it will not work unless one has the same innate talents as the superstar. Attempting to "fake" a talent one doesn't have, or to "catch" it from someone who does, is much like one who is tone-deaf trying to sing or a colorblind person trying to select a color-matched wardrobe.

Natural, God-given talents are like the tiger's stripes—unlike temperament traits, they don't change.

A pair of contrasting stories helps illustrate the two sides of this watershed issue. I (John) was visited by a forty-something Alliance pastor who led a church of more than five hundred members. Everything was going well, he said. But he felt that his ability to lead the church to the next level was lacking, and he was humble enough to admit it. He was open to considering another church if his assessment results pointed in that direction.

Our assessment results provided conclusive information. He appeared to fit a single-cell church better than a multiple-cell church. Five hundred people was over the top for his ideal leadership role. So approaching a smaller church was an option. We also confirmed that he was gifted with the Speaking (preaching) talent—his favorite part of his job.

Then something surprising came up: the talent of Negotiating. He had never considered this, yet it was validated by a strong behavioral pattern dating back to his college days. One of the career advancement options the assessment instrument recommended was that of a mediator for ministry organizations and churches.

It was like a lightning bolt had hit him. He said, "That's it!"

It wasn't but two months before he found a ministry/church mediation consulting firm and was hired. His preaching talent initially attracted him to the pastorate. But now, having completed a successful first fifteen years, he proved submissive to the Lord's direction and followed His guidance into a new chapter.

I also recall a sad situation referred to me by a church. A seminary graduate had been attending the church for some time and was seeking to be mentored by one of the elders, so that he could gain the necessary experience to pastor his own church. The elder became frustrated in the mentoring process because of the individual's inability to perform the tasks assigned to him. The mentoring was transferred to another elder, who met with frustration for the same reasons. This went on for over two years, all parties ending in discouragement and dismay.

The real problem, though, was his unwillingness to place his real talents on the altar.

Finally the would-be pastor was referred to me for an assessment. The appraisal of his aptitudes pointed toward optimal ministry roles other than pastoring. I suggested that he would find greater fulfillment and success in these other roles, where he could use his strengths. He would have nothing to do with my suggestions and returned to the church, complaining that I had not affirmed his pastoral calling. The real problem, though, was his unwillingness to place his real talents on the altar; he refused to submit to God's ideal ministry design for him.

Signs like job dissatisfaction or ongoing conflict with others within one's ministry may be indications that a pastor should reconsider his ideal ministry role. Submission to fresh guidance can't hurt. It might confirm one's current direction, or it might point in a new direction.

District superintendent Jeff Norris tells how the assessment process has helped him focus on his natural talents:

> *I knew I was called of God to serve as a district superintendent, yet I was so overwhelmed by the work of the ministry that I developed hives. After completing the IDAK assessment and having it validated with a trainer, it became evident that one of the A-plus natural talents that God formed in me in my mother's womb was Problem Solving. Discovering this was like beams of light bringing new understanding, new perspectives, and a new energy to so many areas of my life and ministry. I began to see*

how God orchestrated much of my life and past ministries around His giving me the Problem Solving natural talent.

I now lean into this talents; I previously had never read a book on problem solving, but now I study it, refine, and strengthen it. The knowledge and cultivation of this talent has reduced my stress and anxiety and even fostered joy in the midst of difficult situations. I went from dread to peace and even joy.

PS: The hives went away as well.

Willingness and unwillingness to take a second look—these define the two sides of the watershed divide for anyone seeking God's will for his or her ministry career. A valid talent assessment provides part of God's answer to our question, What have You designed me to do? We urge you to make best use of this self-insight for your fruitful ministry future.

Is "Calling" Enough?

Some pastors not only testified to a prompting of God as part of their calling, but also gave evidence of community affirmation and evidence of natural talents. We found that those who sought and found this threefold confirmation of calling were receptive to learn from our assessment model. These individuals had humbly submitted their *chokmah* to God and were at peace about the way God had hardwired them. Their ministry was an adventure, watching how God would provide opportunities for them to lead. They were not following a formula prepared by a superstar. They were not stressed out, striving to show church-growth results. They were content to preach, to do the jobs for which each one has been uniquely equipped and prepared by God. They welcomed the community's guidance and the talent assessment process, giving these influences weight alongside their personal sense of prompting by God.

The one who insists on following a subjective sense of God's "calling," without confirming input from the Christian community and confirming evidence of appropriately suited talents, could be missing a large part of God's message about his or her direction.

Spiritual Gifts and Natural Talents

We found that the topic of spiritual gifts could be an asset or a spoiler, depending on a pastor's interpretation of the biblical passages. If one believed that he must know his spiritual gifts in order to do the job, then he tended to undervalue the important role of God-given natural talents. He would typically assume that he could learn the necessary skills, rather than rely on innate talents. These individuals did not partake in our assessment, nor did they benefit from the coaching and instruction.

I (John) recall the example of one pastor who was referred by his church elders after they had spent over a year working to remedy his leadership flaws, which were hurting the church. He would show up to church ten minutes before starting time and insist on changing the order of service. He would disappear during the week and refuse to answer his cell phone. The pastor claimed that according to his "apostolic calling," he was a pastor-teacher. He blamed the elders for the congregation's complaints and demanded that they resign. The elders asked me to assess the pastor and then spend a couple of sessions with them to provide a plan. I was appalled by the arrogance of the pastor, refusing to acknowledge that he was negligent in the performance of his duties. Yet the pastor's instance that he had the spiritual gift of pastor-teacher made him feel immune to accountability to his elders and congregation.

If you rely solely on discernment of your spiritual gifts for defining your ministry role, you could be missing important components of your complex human makeup, all of which are necessary in order to gain a complete picture of your design. If, however, you consider spiritual gifts along with innate talents, interests, education, and all of the other "suitcases" in your life, then you will gain a more complete picture and will be much more likely to match up with a fulfilling ministry role.

For more information on this issue, read the extended discussion "The Role of Spiritual Gifts" in the preceding chapter.

Bigger Church Size, Same Talents?

Another watershed issue divides those who believe the same leader can lead any size congregation from those who see the need for different talents to lead different size churches. Some would mistakenly claim that a successful pastor of three hundred can just as successfully lead a church of three thousand simply by attending church-growth seminars. Some in this situation did not heed our advice that a large, multiple-cell church needs a multiple-cell senior pastor or executive pastor. The multiple-cell pastor is equipped with one of the Supervisory talents, which enables him to coordinate the many different ministries of the church.

Therefore, a pastor who has the talent to lead a single-cell church (three hundred or fewer) does best to expand the church's impact either by growing and handing leadership to a multiple-cell senior or executive pastor, or by sponsoring daughter churches and keeping the parent church the size in which he is able to love and mentor the people directly.

For more information on this issue, read the extended discussion "Bigger Church Size, Same Talents?" in the preceding chapter.

Is Leadership Learned or Innate?

As we searched for every possible way to reach pastors with the message that they were gifted by a loving God who wanted them to be very successful, we kept bumping into the paradigm that says, *You can learn to be a leader*. Or in different words, You don't need God-given talent to do what you believe you want to do. We wanted to trace the origins of that thinking and came to find that much of it had been fueled by the secular "power of positive thinking" movement led by Napoleon Hill, who claimed, "Whatever the mind conceives, and the heart believes, I can achieve."

> *Much Christian education has come to teach, explicitly or implicitly, the "I can do it" philosophy.*

That unbiblical slogan has subtly crept into our Christian colleges and seminaries, underpinning the mistaken belief that our campuses can teach a person the skills needed to be a pastor. Certainly this is true for someone with the needed innate talents. It also infers that whatever God has not put in you, the school can provide for you. Much Christian education has come to teach, explicitly or implicitly, the "I can do it" philosophy. When surveying promotional literature intended to recruit college students, one reads how a campus promises to make each student a leader, if they will just enroll. Once that "I can do it myself" seed takes root, it can lead the Christian into less-than-productive leadership roles.

Instead, we would urge Christians to seek to understand their innate talents and put them into practice in the leadership roles for which God has uniquely designed each of us.

For more information on this issue, read the extended discussion "Innate or Learned?" in the preceding chapter.

Will God Fill the Talent Gap?

Closely related to the preceding issue is the question of whether or not one buys into the philosophy, "Those whom

God calls, God will equip," which is not scripturally supported. As we discussed in an earlier chapter, this false expectation has sent many men and women into ministry roles for which they are poorly equipped, expecting God to miraculously make up the difference. Nowhere has God made such a promise. Rather, He has lovingly and meticulously designed each individual to fulfill his or her special role in His plan, and He expects us to use our self-awareness—such as that gained through a talents assessment—to help discern His plan for each of us.

Those who dive into an ill-suited ministry role with the expectation of the Lord's "completion" of their equipping are destined for frustration. Those who choose the other side of this watershed are happy to follow where their God-given talents point them.

A Closing Exhortation

If you are a pastor or ministry team member, some of what we have come to believe might be brand new to you. It might challenge some of your assumptions about ministry calling. It might even make you question your decision to enter into the ministry.

It's not our intent at all to discourage or dissuade. In fact, just the opposite! You have been uniquely made by a loving God who has called you. We want our readers to experience the deep satisfaction of discovering that design and then accepting their identity as God's workmanship, doing the specific work for which He designed each one.

And we want you to so fully yield yourself to God—as He uniquely made you—that His Spirit may fill and empower you. He has a purpose and mission for you. We all are called to carry out His Great Commission. And you have a unique niche in that mission that corresponds to your unique composition.

The challenge is not to become something you are not. Too many servants of God try that, some for all of their lives. That path is strewn with frustration, disappointment, and far too many casualties who feel like failures. The real challenge is to come to terms with the way God made you and surrender the right to Him to place you into the right niche.

What holds ministers back from this? Two things: One is not knowing, and the second is fear. If this book motivates you to discover God's innate design, then please don't let fear hold you back. Press on, even if it means change. The value of serving in the right niche will be deeply satisfying to you and glorifying to God.

When we line up our passion to serve with our hardwired talents, we are making music that delights others and, most of all, delights our Maker. I (John) during my visits to see my father at his retirement villa recall being introduced to two pastors who also resided there. As I observed both individuals over time, I found that one continued to reach out to other residents as if he were their pastor. The other, when he was introduced to me, made it clear that he was retired and was no longer fulfilling any part of the pastoral role; there was a chaplain who was hired to do that. Clearly one was a gifted pastor at heart. The other had merely put in his time.

Now that we've discussed these watershed issues, we next come to the work still to be done, the adjustments and improvements so very much needed.

PART V

Adjustments and Improvements

Chapter 11
What Didn't Work

*Joshua son of Nun and Caleb son of Jephunneh ... said to the entire Israelite assembly ... "If the L*ORD *is pleased with us, he will lead us into that land, a land flowing with milk and honey, and will give it to us." (Numbers 14:6-8)*

Failure is a part of God's environment for shaping our character. You cannot fail without risking. If you have never failed, it might just be possible that you have never risked.
—*Erwin McManus,* Seizing Your Divine Moment

Everyone knows that on December 17, 1903, Wilbur and Orville Wright made the first sustained, controlled flight in a powered aircraft on the Atlantic beaches of Kitty Hawk, North Carolina. What's not so well known are the years of struggle and failure before this triumph. By trial and error, the Wright brothers pushed through a series of obstacles—wings that didn't lift, controls that were unreliable, and propellers that broke—until that raw, windy day.

Even then, the 1903 "success" was a straight-line flight of less than a minute. They persisted, however, and by the end of

1905 the Wright Flyer stayed airborne for over half an hour as the brothers flew figure eights over Huffman Prairie, northeast of their hometown of Dayton, Ohio. By 1909 the former bicycle salesmen were selling airplanes commercially, and a new industry was born.

Almost every innovation effort, whether large or small, traces a similar path of stumbles and failures.

Almost every innovation effort, whether large or small, traces a similar path of stumbles and failures. In our case, we had our share. Not everything we tried worked. We've come a long way, and still have more to do.

Gaps in Buy-In

One of our challenges was incomplete buy-in—especially from district leaders and educators. Several factors came into play.

Early on we encountered resistance to the thought of relying on a computerized guidance tool for decisions. Some district leaders preferred instead to rely on gut feelings or intuitive insights when interviewing prospective candidates. Seasoned leaders who had a solid record at placement, of course, saw less need for a new approach. The level of resistance is lower today, though it still surfaces now and then.

In particular, we continue to hear that district offices are reluctant to trust the assessment of another office at face value, in spite of all the success stories. We have carefully evaluated this. Is it the fault of the certification process; are our standards too low? Is this a normal part of human nature, that leaders want the satisfaction of going through the evaluation process themselves? Perhaps a meeting in the middle would be for the second district to conduct a simple process to validate the conclusions of the first, rather than start a new assessment process from scratch.

We also learned about flawed usage of the IDAK tools by some district superintendents and church multiplication leaders. In most instances, these personnel had not completed the full course of C&MA assessment training, or did not master the process through to certification. Online profile results were misinterpreted, which did more harm than good. For example, we learned of interpretations of the instruments that affirmed to the candidate two mutually exclusive talents—such as both a Helping and a Supervisory talent. This misuse completely negated the validity of the interpretation. So quality control issues cropped up despite much effort to keep the bar raised high. We urge all participants to seek complete C&MA certification for the assessment process.

What surfaced more recently is the popularity of well-marketed mass-market profile tools, as the secular world has become convinced of the importance of personality and skill testing for hiring and personnel development. A variety of new tests and profiles gained wide influence. For instance, the Gallup organization's StrengthsFinder books and tests attained instant credibility. The Myers-Briggs personality profile is another well-known tool. A simpler tool is the DISC profile. Some of our field people ran with these approaches to evaluate their candidates.

No precise analysis of these tools has been conducted, yet from an IDAK perspective a simple review finds they do not consistently distinguish personality traits or acquired skills from innate aptitudes that God has given at birth. One of our most important discoveries years ago was the value of separating those factors, not mixing them, for the sake of accurate evaluation. Most importantly, we affirmed the need to identify those innate traits that only God puts in each person.

Furthermore, the possible profiles that emerge in some of the tools are few in number—from a couple dozen down to four (in quadrants). This is a very limiting factor, places all people into too few "buckets," and tends to classify them with relatively nonspecific labels. I (Don) personally witnessed the use of one popular tool by a consultant working with a church board. With no personal knowledge of the members, and with only the results of a twenty-minute inventory, he put the entire group into a category that predicted trouble ahead for their church. This seemed shallow and presumptuous to me, and definitely not constructive for the development of that board. An overly simplistic evaluation became a limitation, if not an outright excuse for emotion-based decisions.

By contrast, the IDAK paradigm acknowledges and honors the value of thousands of unique profiles and affirms how each person contributes to the body of Christ.

Another factor that affected buy-in was the proliferation of assessment tools for use among Christian denominations, especially to evaluate church-planter candidates. In the C&MA, "assessment centers" have been set up in this decade by some districts to assess candidates. Ironically, this method was implemented in the C&MA in the early 1990s, borrowing methodology from the Presbyterian Church of America. About ten centers were established at churches, colleges, and the Alliance seminary. The results were encouraging, but the verdict after three years was that this method was too expensive, too infrequent, and too labor-intensive to be practical for a nationwide planting movement. Those limitations were one reason that we turned to the IDAK approach, since it trained educators and district leaders how to immediately conduct a reliable assessment at their site at relatively low cost.

On campuses, despite our recommendations and support, educators were reluctant to incorporate an aptitude assessment class that would assist with directing ministry candidates to the ministries that best matched their strengths. We will continue similar efforts in the future and urge administrators and teachers to come onboard with us, in the best interests of their students' effective ministry placement and decades of strong kingdom impact.

We also ask educators to reconsider the educational philosophy that leadership talents can be learned. All the evidence shows, instead, that the ministry placement process is heavily dependent on identifying innate talents in ministry candidates and matching them to the best-suited ministry roles.

As a result of the difficulties we've discussed, the implementation of the assessment paradigm throughout the C&MA has been bumpy at times. This book is intended as part of an effort to help all concerned to understand and adopt this paradigm, and we are hopeful for the future.

Complications to Be Simplified

After much of the assessment training had been refined and significantly revised, we began to notice substantial roadblocks that had no easy solutions. Rotation of leadership in each of the district offices and at the national office made continuity difficult. The majority of districts kept the assessment paradigm going through transitions, but a growing number of leaders didn't appear to be using the assessment model to its fullest benefit. I (John) recall sitting with a new assistant vice president who told me that if we were to continue with the assessment model, I needed to come up with something simpler to learn and to use. The old interview system that supplemented the tests and exercises worked fine, but unless a leader used it on a regular basis, his interview skills began to get rusty. Also, I was reminded that the two-part training cycle—first a two-day training, and then later an additional three days—was proving expensive in terms of airfare, motels, and meals.

I needed to go back to the drawing board and develop a new interview process—leaving behind the Cadillac version, yet keeping the process effective, maybe a Chevrolet Impala. The main reason for the long training was the autobiographical interview. It was the elite interview process, and for those district officers who mastered it, they would do no other. When we came up with the Impala version, they were our fiercest critics. But the need for briefer training trumped their objections. The new streamlined process was called the *validation interview*. I had been using it for some time in my secular business training. With modifications, I was able to adapt it to fit the screening of church planters, or any pastor candidate. We kept the key core assumption that the district leaders would use the interview as the final basis for making a placement decision. No test or instrument should replace the seasoned discernment of a district officer. This new adjustment served us well. We then established recertification training for those who had attending the former training but had not chosen to pursue certification.

> **No test or instrument should replace the seasoned discernment of a district officer.**

A few years later I was notified that two psychological tests (the TJTA and the 16PF) had developed an online service. Combining those with the online Talent Discovery Guide, the MAX Report or MAX Profile was born. The benefits are numerous. No longer do districts have to mail answer booklets and wait a week for results. The entire process can be completed in a few days.

We are also making progress toward another simplification—providing an online electronic record of each candidate's assessment, which can be accessed by any district. This will require that districts be willing to take the time to post their results, and also that other districts be willing to trust the results. Yet this is a major step forward. A related beneficial step is the posting of assessments of students coming up through each of the Alliance campuses.

The Ones That Got Away

Fishermen talk of the big catches that got away. We found that we, too, missed potential multiplication leaders.

The dream of building a system of recruitment and assessment campus-wide at C&MA schools did not flesh out. For various reasons, the campus reps didn't prioritize actively recruiting church-planter candidates (those with the Initiating/Developing talent).

What is more, some who fit the planter profile do not excel in traditional educational programs, nor do they have much patience with extended assessment and evaluation periods. They may even drop out of school partway through. Spotting and appreciating such individuals among the student body takes a person with an eye to see beyond these maverick tendencies to the potential that lies untapped.

I (John) recall sitting in classes led by scholarly professors, yet not motivated by the curriculum. How did this class apply to my future? I knew my future direction, so it was easy for me to evaluate courses that did or did not fit my direction. I needed to graduate, but perhaps didn't need to get As and Bs in courses that didn't apply. I felt sympathy for the pastoral students who, not knowing any better, were admonished to excel in all classes in order to be fully prepared for the rigors of the pastorate. Sadly, each professor had his own views of what it took to succeed as a pastor, so the student was pulled in multiple directions without realizing it. How refreshing to these students would be a unified message from all concerned encouraging them to seek reliable self-assessment, so they could more wisely narrow the focus of their academic efforts?

Amazing to us, districts are reluctant to recruit students from non-C&MA campuses that hold to compatible doctrinal beliefs. Certainly some such recruiting is going on, but so much more can be done on the part of campus development officers and district officers. Since we recognize that church planters are so rare, it would seem that the net of recruitment should be getting larger rather than staying in the same fishing pools.

Another pool in which to seek and find planter candidates is among successful midcareer baby boomers. Throughout the body of Christ are those who have been successful in entrepreneurial business careers, and who are ready in their forties or fifties to switch tracks. Moving into full-time ministry is realistic and attractive option for them. Some of them are wired to be church planters, their Supervisory talents having already been honed and developed through their earlier career experience. We need to stop letting these talented individuals slip through the cracks in our recruiting efforts. We recommend establishing assessment centers on campus for midcareer individuals who might serve their remaining effective decades in a ministry career. These assessment centers could also serve alumni who want to return for a midcareer change of direction.

> *Another pool in which to seek and find planter candidates is among successful midcareer baby boomers.*

Forthcoming Improvements

The Alliance has a wonderful application process for pastor candidates. Candidates are prescreened and preapproved by the district offices before they are referred to a church. Once approved in one district, a candidate is eligible for placement anywhere in United States. This eliminates much duplication and standardizes the requirements for church ministry across the board.

However, many churches find themselves reinventing the wheel every time they need to screen the candidates provided by the district superintendent. We hope to produce a simple packaged "kit," including audio or video instruction and coaching, to assist the search committee. This would save the district office many hours, save the search committee some agony, and help identify the best candidate for the job.

On a different front, culturally sensitive online testing and interview systems have just begun to be implemented. During 2014 this issue was explored, systems tested, and a new process introduced for 2015, which would allow all multicultural districts to assess pastors for their culture using their own language and cultural priorities.

Among future issues, we look forward to fleshing out unexpected surprises that have come along—the topic of our next chapter.

Chapter **12**
What We Learned

Pass on what you heard from me—the whole congregation
saying Amen!—to reliable leaders who are competent to
teach others. (2 Timothy 2:2, MSG)

Teamwork comes down to mastering a set of behaviors
that are at once theoretically uncomplicated, but extremely
difficult to put into practice day after day. Success comes
only for those groups that overcome the all-too-human
behavioral tendencies that corrupt teams and breed
dysfunctional politics within them.
—Patrick Lencioni, The Five Dysfunctions of a Team

We have not arrived! In this chapter we share lessons
learned—some the hard way—but we see a constant need to
adapt our assessment tools and processes to new realities. This
reflects our conviction that churches and denominations must
strive to be "learning organizations."

In business, executives hope their companies will thrive by
creating or acquiring knowledge a little faster than their competition. In the church, the motive for learning is not to beat

the competition, it's to meet the changing culture on its terms with an unchanging gospel.

Here is some of what we've learned so far, and hints as to where we go next.

Generational Continuity

For several reasons, it's challenging to embed any new procedure or process in a culture such as the C&MA. First, autonomy is an underlying value at the local church and district level. Almost any centralized strategy or process is viewed as a one-size-fits-all answer. The first reaction is to question it.

Second, most tools used in the field have a short shelf life. Most of us have bookshelves cluttered with notebooks that only gather dust. At one time, each of those seminars or programs seemed like the next great idea, or at least the solution to a nagging problem. To be honest, most of these are never implemented. And the ones that are used last a few years before fading into obscurity. Any tool that beats those odds is a rare exception. Showing that this assessment process was one of the exceptions was part of our challenge.

Third, there is turnover in leadership, both in the national office staff and in the twenty-eight district offices. Since 1991, there have been six vice presidents of Church Ministries and five denominational presidents. New leaders cycle in with an amazing variety of experiences and opinions. The continual "restocking" of leaders brings needed creativity and freshness. But it makes it more difficult to sustain a strategy across the seasons of change.

Fourth is the sheer effort it takes to orient and train each succeeding administration at the national and district levels. Only leaders with longevity and credibility can recruit other leaders to implement an assessment tool across the board.

Looking back, we find it remarkable that a tool put into service more than two decades ago is fully useful today—even more than before, given the adjustments we've made.

The longevity in the field through the cycles of denominational leaders is due to several things. Most of the credit goes to the proven value of the process. It would have gone nowhere without positive results. Stories abound of how well-implemented assessments have confirmed church-planter candidates.

In my (Don's) first month as superintendent in Minnesota, Tim contacted me expressing interest in the possibility of planting a new church under the Alliance in the Twin Cities. That is not the usual phone call a superintendent receives! So of course I followed up with him. Tim's profile demonstrated clear evidence of a Supervisory talent, together with a set of other talents highly conductive for planting. He was available before we had a place for him to plant. So we hired him to do a detailed demographic study that would identify the most needy places in the Twin Cities for a new church plant. He came back within weeks with a bound notebook, census projections, housing information, and church attendance by community. All on his own.

We gave Tim his choice to go to either of the best two locations. He made his choice and with district backing moved in and began the hard work of gathering a core group. One of our churches partnered with him and released a couple of families to join the effort. It was only months until Tim had established a core group. In less than a year the church went public with worship services at a rented location. They quickly established ministries, training of leaders, outreach, and evangelism, and organized a leadership board. Ahead of schedule, the church weaned itself from supplemental funds and became a fully accredited C&MA church. Today it is thriving and seeking a permanent facility.

My point? Among other things, I'm glad that I, as a brand-new superintendent, had a ready-made process for assessing Tim's talent profile. I didn't have to depend on my gut to guess whether he would be suitable as a church planter.

> *I didn't have to depend on my gut to guess whether he would be suitable as a church planter.*

Other stories tell of an assessment turning up certain talents in a person that masqueraded as the aptitude for startups. While I served in Michigan, a potential candidate applied who was absolutely convinced he possessed the qualities for a church planter. In conversation he was articulate, persuasive, promotional, energetic, connected. There was a Bible study meeting in his home—all evidences that seemed to support his claim.

In earlier days I might have been so impressed as to buy in on the basis of his self-presentation. However, I held back and began probing with questions. When I asked for examples of his initiating new ministries, projects, businesses, community groups, sports teams—anything—he could not offer one clear instance. He could certainly speak well and promote well, but the Initiating/Developing talent was not documented at all. In fact the group meeting in his home, I discovered, was made up mostly of people who had left another church together.

So at the end of a series of conversations I broke the news to him that we would not be moving further with him in the direction of church planting. At that point, he responded angrily that I was wrong and was missing something God wanted done. If I needed confirmation of my decision, his response alone was it.

Did I make a mistake? I believe God saved me from one. In fact, this careful process likely did this man a favor and also saved funds that would otherwise have been wasted on a failed or crippled startup.

Strong advocates for this assessment paradigm have remained over the years in positions of influence in the denomination. Sometimes in national roles and sometimes in district roles, these voices helped tell the story, promote the training, and highlight positive results.

Protecting the Soldier

Pastoral ministry is a demanding responsibility. A variety of tasks go with the territory—from preaching to counseling, from administration to fundraising. Expectations are connected to each task, and pastors are evaluated on how well they do with this broad range of duties. (*CNNMoney* rated minister as the tenth-most-stressful job. With low pay![8])

Even the multitalented pastor faces a plethora of high expectations. And for those with servant hearts but limited abilities, the expectations seem impossible to meet. No pastor escapes criticism, but the sad fact is that a certain percentage will eventually be fired.

I (Don) have personally worked with men who gave evidence of a divine call, showed godly character, and loved people deeply, but nevertheless were terminated from a pastorate within just a few years. In a number of those situations, the problem was not moral failure, anger issues, or other justified reasons for removal, but sub-par performance in relation to expectations of the church leaders. For example, a pastor with a preaching style that does not connect with his congregation, or who exercises inadequate pastoral care to senior adults, or who lacks a clearly articulated direction. In too many of these cases the fact is that the church and pastor never matched up well.

Consider the pastor whose primary aptitudes are suited for giving support and care, whose personality is gentle and warm, and who has the spiritual gift of mercy. Yes, of course, certain churches need that kind of pastor. But some churches are a mismatch for that profile. For example, those that need firm directional leadership to deal with a longstanding sin issue or seething conflict. The pastor with the shepherd-style profile may become exhausted by trying to resolve conflict. His gentle style, which served well in a previous church, becomes the very target for criticism in this one. I've seen such pastors wounded deeply, and often not because of any failure on their part, but because of a mismatch with the church.

> *The toll a mismatch exacts is severe, not only on the pastor, but on the spouse and any children in the home.*

The toll a mismatch exacts is severe, not only on the pastor, but on the spouse and any children in the home. Often the pastor is haunted by a sense of failure, anger, self-doubt, and anxiety about the future and the possibility of firing. The church might not fare any better, especially after a firing. It can lose people who did click with the pastor, or who received meaningful ministry from him. If a long interim ensues, the church might lose any momentum it had.

In one case, a dominant founding pastor led a church to grow to over three hundred and through several building phases. But his style of tightly holding the reins led to a season of tension and wrestling—and eventually to his departure. As often happens, the board swung the pendulum all the way over when they called the next pastor. He was gentle, compassionate, and deliberate. A deep spiritual life manifested in his prayer ministry and biblical teaching. Not surprisingly, people flocked to him for counseling.

These strengths were welcomed and helped the church recover. But after that, the need shifted from healing and helping to vision and planning for the future. The pressure mounted for him to establish a clear direction for the future. Sadly, when a sure word was needed, he vacillated, uncertain where to take them or how to get there. Various solutions were proposed and pulled back. Frustration among lay leaders mounted to the point that confidence was fatally damaged, and finally he was asked to resign. The ending was not positive, and a good brother was wounded. This end was not brought on by heretical teaching, moral failure, or some other grievous cause. Instead, as we discovered the hard way, it was a classic example of a pastoral profile that was ideal for an interim healing ministry, but was not suited for taking the church to the next level once it recovered.

So what can be done to help pastors several years into a pastorate, *before* a termination? The truth is that if everyone denies the gathering clouds, they will not reach out for help from an overseer or take it when offered. In those cases, it is tough for the overseer to do more than stay close and hope for a change of mind.

Fortunately, many pastors today seek help and accept it from their denomination. Especially if word gets out that the denomination cares and is proactive. For us, it was an aspiration at first, then eventually a deeply held conviction, that the C&MA should and could help its own pastors. This is another reflection of our core commitment to steward the people God gives.

We set out to apply assessment tools to the pastor who's not in the right church. If we can help a pastor move into a church that is a good match, everyone wins—the pastor and family, and the new church. Given a fresh start, pastors can take off, thrive, and be fruitful. Sometimes a better fit is found in an associate staff position, rather than lead pastor.

But how do you make that match? On the church's part, it involves a clear and realistic consensus among the lay leaders about the two or three essential A-plus qualities to seek in their next pastor. On the pastor's part, it involves discovery through assessment of his top strengths and personality traits. And on the district overseer's part, it means doing the time-consuming work of knowing the churches' needs, and evaluating candidates well. Matches that are made in heaven can be confirmed on earth through careful assessment.

We also discovered the need to help some pastors consider a shift to a different ministry track altogether, outside the local church. In such cases, the best counsel is not about serving at another church. It is to honor God's call and express it in other Christian ministries outside the pastorate.

For example, the hypothetical shepherding pastor described above is in fact a person most district leaders have met. In my (Don's) experience, lots of pastors are wired primarily to extend a shepherd's care. Some struggle in every church they have. The typical criticism is that they are not effective leaders or administrators. We've been able to help some work out reasonable expectations with a specific congregation that primarily desires shepherding. Happily, those "marriages" last a long time. But I've come alongside several of them—not with the verdict that they'll never serve in ministry, but with the suggestion to step into, say, a chaplaincy role where their helping talents can be put into practice at least 60 percent of the time. Some have taken the risk of changing tracks in middle age. Their call can be fulfilled, their gifts and talents utilized, and their lives fruitful. This is anything but failure. It is glorifying God by serving in the roles for which He made them!

> *Some struggle in every church they have.*

Recognizing the Human Element

No assessment is perfect. No assessment can predict with certainty how a person will do, even in a position that fits well. It's not possible.

God's servants are forgiven and redeemed, to be sure, but still imperfect human beings. And we live and serve in a sinful world under the domination of the evil one. The effects of sin are all around. Not only that, sin can rear its ugly head within God's servants.

So even the most careful assessment can be undermined. Promising candidates can choose to stray and disobey. That path derails them from the ministry trajectory they could have experienced through obedience and the Spirit's fullness.

I (Don) think of two very talented candidates who were assessed to be among the few who are wired to be pioneer church planters. The divergence after several years was startling. One continued on the way of obedience and sanctification. He steadily developed a new church from a handful to more than 150, still meeting in a cramped rented facility while searching for a permanent location. The one who yielded to sin issues within his temperament struggled to establish a core group, alienated people who were offended, and tragically lost his marriage.

Talent was not the difference. It was a spiritual difference that took one up and another down. This points out one of the intangibles that assessment cannot determine with certainty.

Another human element is the tendency to override or even ignore the results of an objective assessment. Information is provided to the decision makers. But the opposite decision is made in spite of it. In a purely objective context, this would not happen. But we operate in a human context. So information is not always decisive. In our case, we found that sometimes candidates were placed as planters contrary to the assessment's findings.

This kind of thing happened (and still does) for very human reasons. The placement supervisor may strongly desire to place a certain person as a planter who has strengths in promotion (self-promotion perhaps), or bonds easily and quickly with people. The positive impression and observation so strongly inclines the placement person that it overrides the absence of the Initiating/Developing talent strength. In some situations, the Multi-Relational talent causes the interviewer to instantly like the candidate, and the interviewer begins looking for what is positive about the candidate rather than objectively evaluating strengths. Also, the Acting talent can sometimes equip the candidate to size up the interviewer and quickly adjust to whatever the job requires, appearing to have all the traits needed.

Relationship webs also influence decisions. If there is an old-boy network, then its members may be favored over unknown but better-qualified candidates. Or graduates of a certain college or seminary may get preferential placement. Even a family name or reputation can weigh more heavily. We have seen all of these factors at work.

Still another human factor is how the person assessed responds to the outcome. A strongly held personal identity is a powerful internal force. Let's say that a pastor has struggled in three churches in a row; the reason is the same—say, preaching is not a strength, and is the target for criticism and people leaving. So an assessment suggests that a ministry outside the pastorate would be a better fit—for example, a Christian camp staff position that does not require upfront presenting. Objectively, that person would be more energized and probably fruitful there. But internally, the pastor has twenty years of experience and has wrapped his self-identity around being a pastor. He's reluctant to change because change feels frightening. Either it is too painful to think of leaving what he knows, or a role outside the church would totally conflict with his identity. In the end, the pastor says thank you for the assessment but ignores its implications.

We've learned that assessment is a tool. It offers an objective and informed opinion. It is vastly superior to hunches, first impressions, and wishful thinking. But the human beings who receive the results must still make the final decisions.

What can you do about the human element? As you may have influence and opportunity, continue to emphasize personal purity and honesty among those within your sphere of responsibility. You may find yourself with the opportunity to save a ministry, a marriage, or a life. And make it your habit to search your own heart, in case the Holy Spirit might reveal one of these human shortcomings within you and seek to lead you in His way everlasting.

Exceptions to the Rule

Whenever there are rules, we usually find exceptions. We found two very big exceptions.

The first relates to the apparently unequivocal need for the Initiator/Developer talent for church planting. Except ... with the especially gifted preaching pastors, who gather a crowd no matter where they speak. All they need is a room, and in a few months there will be a gathering. People are so attracted to the speaker that they joyfully step up and do what needs to be done to fill in the void. That has happened in many places, but it is the exception, not the rule. One cannot count on it.

> *Whenever there are rules, we usually find exceptions.*

I (John) recall a contemporary, highly gifted preacher who said that he requested to plant a church in his denomination, and they turned him down. Later he just started preaching and the people came by the truckload. Today he is one of the top ten preachers in the U.S. This illustration is further enhanced by the observation that when the leader enjoys trust and respect, the congregation voluntarily steps forward and fills the voids to make their revered leader look good. Yet this is the exception, not the rule. One should not plan for this kind of trust and respect from others; it may come and it may not.

We witnessed a second exception to the rule during a training session at the Alliance office. During that training cycle we would videotape trainees doing their candidate interviews with live practicum candidates. In one particular video session, while the rest of us were watching via closed circuit broadcast, an elderly missionary was being interviewed regarding his Relational talents. The interview was going very well, and the pattern of relational behavior was strongly suggesting a Singular Relational talent. Then out of nowhere the individual began sharing enjoyable experiences that were more common to the Familiar Group and even Multi-Relational talents. *How could this be?* I wondered. The elderly gentleman didn't need to impress us; he was a proven warrior. Yet he was clearly out of character, a different person in his old age.

And that was it. I realized that I was observing one who was living out the fruit of the Spirit. And as this growing, glowing fruit (manifesting as positive temperament traits) grew more fragrant in his life, he began to give forth a sweet aroma—that is, behaviors attributed to talents that were not part of his original design. This was not the rule, but a blessed exception. I have marveled at that example and have found a few others like this man in the years since that experience. I only hope to become one of those who also brings forth the aroma of the fruit of the Spirit as an encouragement to others.

> **I realized that I was observing one who was living out the fruit of the Spirit.**

On the Horizon

Two additional prospects are on the horizon, but within reach. Both are opportunities to take our system to the next level.

First, though there are trained assessors in many C&MA districts, valid assessment results don't always make it into the licensing pipeline. In other words, assessment and accreditation are not yet linked. It would deepen the quality of both if they were connected.

The desired scenario is that every candidate applicant in which every district takes serious interest would undergo the same kind of assessment. The interviewing and placement leaders would all have access to the results in the form of a MAX Report, which would form the basis for guidance and placement. Furthermore, in the ordination preparation process prior to placement, the mentor or mentoring group would utilize the MAX Report to personalize their guidance to the licensing and ordination council.

This would give the advantage of eliminating or at least reducing the duplication of assessment that exists now. Each district would use a common language and paradigm to evaluate candidates' ministry prospects. And there would be a basis for interdistrict communication on candidates.

The second opportunity is to start sooner. Why wait for assessment until the candidates are in the hands of districts? Why not get that done earlier? Alliance colleges and the seminary have been reluctant to embed an aptitude assessment into their student development systems. Granted, it is a nontraditional element of education, but one that has been needed. A few baby steps have been taken, but so much more could be done. The value should be obvious, and we urge educators at all levels to encourage this development.

I (John) speak, not in theory, but from experience. Witness, for example, the success gained by Dr. Mark O'Farrell, a former Alliance district superintendent who was appointed as president of Trinity College in Florida (a non-Alliance campus). One week after his appointment, I received a call asking me to fly out to Florida and set up a talent-based assessment system for his students. After ten years that program continues today, run by the school's own faculty.

My experiences with multiple campuses is that universities are more reluctant to guide their students to a meaningful vocation; they leave that up to the student. On the other hand, Bible colleges and seminaries, together with campuses that train future ministry leaders, are more inclined to be concerned about the successful placement of their students. Yet, in all, we continue to see generations being educated but poorly equipped to find their future calling.

I recall a definitive moment in the history of Denver Seminary. Then-president Dr. Haddon Robinson had experienced "the final straw" complaint from a church who had hired one of his graduates. Apparently the graduate was accused of child molestation. That triggered an effort to do a more responsible job of assessing each student, so as to provide proper guidance for a wise ministry choice. I got involved, and for twenty years every student was required to meet with Tom Board, a local counselor, for three hours. He performed the IDAK assessment and then followed each student each year, noting his or her progress and eventual selection of a ministry career. The campus further tailored the student's field education requirement to affirm the ministry career selection. It was the Cadillac of all the campus student assessment programs in which I have participated. Each student was given a unique opportunity to start his or her service for the King on the right foot. This continued until several leadership changes in senior management led them to adopt a different program.

We believe it would be a great value to ministry students to undergo an assessment process early in their scholastic preparation, especially as a prerequisite for field education placement. In addition to acquiring a degree, students would acquire self-understanding of how God has made them and the possible types of ministry for which they are designed. Graduates who would approach districts for placement with this information already in hand would definitely strengthen their prospects. It could facilitate the job of district leaders who place new people. We believe that those schools that add this element of preparation for their students will definitely enhance the students' placement potential.

Chapter 13
Conclusion: Looking Forward

We are God's workmanship, created in Christ Jesus to do good works, which God prepared in advance for us to do. (Ephesians 2:10)

All enterprises or projects, big or small, begin in the mind's eye, they begin with imagination and with the belief that what is merely an image can one day be made real.
—*James Kouzes and Barry Posner,* The Leadership Challenge

Well, that's our story. You may already be part of it. Or maybe you're just now considering joining it. Or taking the next step.

This book contains dozens of possible applications, and we encourage you to refer back to it in order to consider the part you will fulfill in your circles of influence. At the very least, please consider implementing the following action points:

- Celebrate that you are a unique creation of God, that He did not make a mistake when He made you.

- Take the risk of reaching out to pursue your own personal talent assessment. Contact the IDAK Group *(www.idakgroup.com)*, where you will find talent assessment instruments you can complete, as well as a list of our preferred counselors with pictures and bios.

- Prayerfully build a personal ministry "craft" that employs your talent strengths at least 60 percent of the time.

- Bring the assessment tool into your circle of influence—your board, your church staff, your district, your school ...

- Tell your friends and colleagues what you discover.

And dream with us. Imagine your church, your denomination, your country, your world in the years to come, when the theology and practice of Bible-based personal assessment becomes better understood and more widely implemented. The dream begins with ministers-in-training learning their unique design by God, with colleges and seminaries that include personal assessment in their curriculum, internships, and career placement offices. It continues with pastors-in-practice understanding themselves as made by God, accepting His talents and gifts rather than wishing to be someone else. With staff teams discovering their unique design and humbly seeking to complement one another and work together as parts of a fully functioning body. With lay leaders accepting the mix of talent strengths and gifts their leaders have been given, rather than criticizing them for what they have not been given.

Imagine the time savings and assurance for regional leaders alone as they place church leaders with confidence and nationwide cooperation.

Picture hundreds of new church planters and church-planting teams raised up around the country, yielding hundreds of new and healthy churches. Envision with us the thousands of people from multiple ethnicities who will be reached with the gospel and become wholehearted disciples of Jesus Christ.

And dream of the world we will change.

APPENDIX

Temperament and Talent Traits in Church Ministry

Definitions for **Temperament and Talent Traits in the MAX Profile Report**

PRIMARY TEMPERAMENT TRAITS

1. **Tested Character:** Person demonstrates a tested faith, has encountered sufficient crisis experiences that have tested their convictions, values, and faith. Standing by convictions may have cost this person financially or cost friendships, reputation, job, and the like.

2. **Appropriate Self-Esteem:** Person demonstrates a positive self-image, "can do" attitude, confidence to try something new or difficult, not afraid to fail, attracts confident competent others.

3. **Self-Discipline:** Person demonstrates an ability to stay focused, perseveres to complete a preset goal; self-directed, persistence.

4. **Optimism:** Person sees present or future in a positive way; looks first to the positive potential of difficult issues, projects, and events. The opposite of this trait is Depression, which is all too common for pastors.

5. **Team Player:** Trusting of others, respect for others, giving up personal preferences for benefit of team, affirms others.

SECONDARY TEMPERAMENT TRAITS

For Secondary Traits, only those scores that suggest problematic traits are reported. These undesirable traits are noted as appearing to need additional evaluation. The MAX Report considers twenty-seven Secondary Traits. An individual may have no Secondary Trait Scores that appear to need additional evaluation. Traits marked with an asterisk (*) are to be considered as most troublesome for achieving peak job performance.

Adventure-Seeking-Low: Person may be exceedingly cautious and restrained in taking risks; person may want to continually rehearse what to do rather than take the risk of being embarrassed.

Adventure-Seeking-High: Person may seek exceedingly high excitement or adrenalin rushes. Person may be addicted to the pursuit of activities that are socially taboo, seeking out socially bold, dangerous, or risky ventures.

*Assertive-High: Person may demonstrate exceedingly high assertiveness, which may result in dominant or competitive behavioral patterns, resulting in overpowering others and squelching others' contributions.

Cautious, Introspection-High: Person may have a pattern of being sober, serious, or fearful regarding events and circumstances before taking action.

*Compliant-High: Person appears to be exceedingly low in assertiveness, which may result in a more passive, compliant, dependent, or submissive behavioral pattern.

Composure-Low: Person appears to be exceedingly low in composure. This means that this person may have a pattern of being nervous, apprehensive, stressed, or anxious.

Diplomatic, Forthright-High: Person scored exceedingly low in diplomacy, therefore resulting in being forthright without restraint. Person may make statements that could offend others in public, saying the first thing that comes to mind, sometimes referred to as "foot in mouth."

Diplomatic, Masked-High: Person scored exceedingly high in being shrewd and masked. Person may manipulate others so that no one really knows his or her true motives.

Established, Tradition-High: Person scored exceedingly high regarding a strong adherence to established customs, traditions, beliefs and procedures; person may remain too long in abusive relationships and working conditions because of inappropriate loyalty.

Experimentation and Change-High: Person scored exceedingly high in the need for continuous experimentation and change, may have difficulty maintaining loyalty and long-term relationships.

Exuberance-High: Person scored exceedingly high in exuberance and is inclined to only see the bright side of life. Person may paint an inappropriate rosy picture when addressing grief, death, and painful life situations.

*Flexing with Setbacks-Low: Person scored exceedingly low in being able to quickly adjust to unpredictable events or emergencies. This means that when experiencing an emergency, person may lose the ability to maintain composure or not be able to take quick action during an unexpected setback.

Flexing with Setbacks-High: Person scored exceedingly high in adjusting to the unexpected, which may result in an attraction to last-minute or spur-of-the-moment activities.

Initiating Conversation-Low: Person scored exceedingly low in his or her desire to initiate conversation with people and thus may appear cold, aloof, or distant.

Initiating Conversation-High: Person scored exceedingly high in his or her desire to begin a conversation with people and thus may seek to please to an excess.

Learning Abstract Concepts-High: Person scored exceedingly high in intellectual reasoning ability and may need a continued high intellectual challenge in order to be fulfilled in job duties with a minimum of repetitious duties.

*Learning Concrete Concepts-High: Person scored exceedingly high for concrete learning, which may result in learning only by doing through repetition, demonstration, and trial and error. Person may be confused or distracted when instructed with intangible concepts, theories, or procedures.

Nervous Tension-High: Person scored exceedingly high regarding anxiety or nervous tension. This means that he or she may have trouble relaxing.

*Objective Decision-Making-Low: Person scored exceedingly low for objective decision-making, which may result in more emotional or intuitive-based decisions and few, if any, logical reason-based decisions.

Objective Decision-Making-High: Person scored exceedingly high in objective decision-making ,which may result in a lack of feelings, intuition, or emotion applied to decision-making.

Perfectionism-High: Person scored exceedingly high regarding perfectionism. This means that he or she may demand exceedingly high standards for self or others.

*Relaxation-High: Person scored exceedingly high in being laid back, showing very low anxiety and nervous tension; person may be very laid back during a crisis or lack ambition.

Socially Active-Low: Person scored exceedingly low in social interaction and thus may be withdrawn, quiet, or removed from social interaction.

Suppressed Communication of Inner Feelings-High: Person scored exceedingly high in suppressing inner feelings, which may result in restrained, unresponsive, or repressed communication with others.

*Sympathy-Low: Person scored exceedingly low for sympathy, which may result in insensitive, unfeeling, or inconsiderate communication or behavior.

*Intolerance, Anger-High: Person scored exceedingly high for intolerance, which may result in being too critical, angry, impatient, hostile, or intolerant of other's mistakes and weaknesses.

Tolerance for Disorder-High: Person scored exceedingly high in tolerating disorder. This means that he or she may have low performance standards for self and for others.

NATURAL TALENTS (in alphabetical order)

Communicational Talents (conveying a mood, feeling, or idea):

Acting/Imitating Mannerisms: Modifying one's behavior and attitudes to portray a defined character. Adaptable to cross-cultural encounters.

Broadcasting/Telephone: Conveying information, moods, or feelings through verbal discussion using the telephone, video broadcasting, radio broadcasting, or other audio/visual media.

Composing/Arranging Music: Expressing a mood or feeling through music via written composition.

Conversing: Generating and sustaining an easy flow of one-to-one discussion resulting in a sense of mutual understanding.

Designing: Expressing moods, ideas, or concepts through design layouts including graphic arts, architecture, drafting, landscape, drawing, and the like.

Giving Presentations with Audience Interaction: Giving presentations in front of others that include audience interaction such as management briefings, workshops, seminars, giving announcements, or performing the role of a master of ceremonies.

Giving Speeches: Persuasively and accurately presenting information, moods, or feelings through the use of the spoken word targeted to a live audience.

Group Moderating: Facilitating group discussion or group interaction.

Painting: Expressing moods, feelings, or concepts through painting with oils, pastels, chalk, and the like; does not necessarily include detailed design.

Singing or Instrumental Performing: Performing before an audience through the means of singing or instrument playing.

Teaching by Lecture: Presenting information in an easily understandable way to a group. The emphasis is on audience understanding.

Using Colors and Patterns: Expressing moods or feelings through the arrangement of colors, patterns, fabrics, or textures such as in clothing, wallpaper, photography, or silk screening.

Using Handcrafts: Expressing a mood or feeling through the creation of jewelry or other craft items made of wood, leather, cloth, or other materials.

Using Shapes and Forms: Expressing moods or feelings through the arrangement of objects, shapes, or undefined forms, including room arrangement, architectural landscaping, housing, or urban planning, and sculpture.

Writing Words: Clearly conveying information, moods, or feelings through the use of written words.

Relational Talents (amount of time to form a trust bond with a new acquaintance):

Familiar Group Relational: Developing rapport with individuals through repeated contact (nine to twelve months to bond).

Multi-Relational: Quickly establishing rapport with all types of people on first encounters (minutes or hours to bond).

Singular Relational: Developing rapport over an extended period of time (three-plus years to bond).

Functional Talents (task-oriented aptitudes):

Analyzing to Understand: Examining, dissecting, or contemplating a given concept, subject matter, or object in order to understand its component parts and interrelationships.

Appraising/Estimating: Appraising the monetary value of almost anything or judging the feasibility of a proposed idea, new venture, or new product.

Being of Service (Nurturing): Helping others to achieve their goals and meet their needs.

Being Physically Coordinated or Physically Active: Overall physical activity including use of arms, body, and legs in a skillful, coordinated fashion.

Calculating Numbers: Quickly and accurately performing numerical computations such as percentages, arithmetic functions, or statistical probabilities; may also include accounting and bookkeeping.

Classifying: Efficiently classifying, filing, storing information so it can be retrieved easily.

Counseling (Nurturing): Sensitively evaluating individual needs, desires, or dreams and encouraging resolution of problems and conflicts.

Creating: Forming new associations among previously unrelated concepts, objects, or systems. Continually experimenting or tinkering with new ideas.

Evaluating People's Character: Discerning people's character quickly and accurately.

Imagining: Forming new associations in one's mind through theorizing, philosophizing, daydreaming, hypothesizing, developing story characters, and so forth.

Initiating/Developing New Ventures: The capacity to recruit people to a vision and to oversee the startup efforts to accomplish the vision.

Inventing: Developing new technical equipment and/or electrical systems. Can also include developments in wood, concrete, plastic, or glass.

Long-Range Logistical Planning: Projecting one's thinking into the long-range future to determine scheduling details, sequence of events, resources needed, potential problems, reserves necessary for emergencies, and hidden costs, as related to a group project.

Making Future Projections: Predicting future trends, opinions, or fads, as related to politics, social and cultural trends, and the like.

Managing Established Groups, Organizations: Coordinating the ongoing efforts and activities of others in achieving a common goal, encouraging each individual to make his or her maximum contribution.

Mechanical/Technical Troubleshooting: Discovering the source of a mechanical/electrical/ technical failure or breakdown.

Negotiating: Grasping the needs and/or desires of at least two unrelated persons or groups, finding a common denominator in both and uniting all in the agreement of a defined goal, idea, or project.

Observing in Three Dimensions: Seeing a three-dimensional object or building from a two-dimensional drawing, including mechanical drawings, blueprints, maps, or aerial photographs.

Observing Physical Environment: Noticing visual detail in one's surroundings.

Observing Printed Details: Noticing visual detail in blueprints, maps, legal documents, technical manuals, and the like.

Operating/Driving: Skillfully coordinating pedals, levers, computer keyboard and mouse, or steering systems simultaneously so as to effectively run equipment machinery, helicopters, automobiles, and the like.

Ordering Personal Space: Maintaining things in their proper place, maintaining established procedures and rules, sensing the most efficient positioning of materials for easy retrieval.

Ordering Personal Time and Priorities: Ordering one's own schedule to reflect what is the most important task at any given time and how long it will take.

Promoting: Directly or indirectly motivating another's thoughts or behavior towards acceptance of a subject matter, opinion, or persons.

Quick Reflex Action: Quickly reacting to an immediate physical emergency and making a fast, responsible decision.

Reassuring and Supporting (Nurturing): Individually empathizing with another's hurts, frustrations, or anxieties.

Recording and Auditing: Counting and recording individual items or numerical values in a precise, accurate manner; may also include accounting and bookkeeping.

Remembering: Tallying, recording and quickly recalling details from memory.

Researching/Investigating: Seeking, gathering, or probing for information involving multiple resources concerning a certain subject matter or object.

Selling: Introducing a concept or object in a manner acceptable to an individual or group so as to result in a sale. Includes recruiting volunteers and fundraising.

Solving Problems: Discovering the source of an error (human logic) or diagnosing underlying causes.

Synthesizing: Examining ideas, elements, or concepts in order to bring them together to form a whole.

Taking Risks: Being productive where the successful outcome of future programs, investments, or expenditures is unknown.

Tutoring (Nurturing): Assisting others one-on-one in overcoming learning problems or disabilities.

Using One's Hands and Arms: Physical activity, including use of one's hands and arms in a coordinated fashion, including skillful use of tools while repairing, assembling, sewing, hammering nails, and the like.

Using One's Hands and Fingers: Precise, detailed physical activity of one's hands and fingers in a skilled, coordinated fashion.

PRIORITY TALENTS FOR PASTORS

Communicational Talents—Any one of the following:

Speaking (Preaching). Most preferred.

Teaching.

Acting. This talent will significantly enhance but not substitute for the above two talents; an excellent talent for youth pastors and for multiethnic churches.

Acting with **Writing.** Dramatic sermon reading; can be substituted for Speaking or Teaching talent.

Relational Talents—Any one of the following:

Multi-Relational. For a three hundred-plus and growing church.

Familiar Group. For any size church.

Singular Relational. Only if Speaking (preaching) talent is strong, not for a church in or recovering from conflict, not for a church of less than one hundred, unless the pastor was raised in or knows the church well.

Functional Talents—Any of the thirty-six Functional talents will be an asset. Following are special comments on some of these:

Time and Priorities. One of the most preferred Functional talents, as it indicates that a candidate will be efficient with his time and very productive.

Order of Space. Indicates an orderly and organized work style. It favors following policies, procedures, and tradition. It does not favor change. Not an appropriate talent for youth pastors.

Creative. Favors change, innovation and experimentation. This talent is not recommended for an established, traditional, structured church. This talent is not the *change-agent* talent. An excellent talent for youth pastors.

Supervisory Talents—Each of this cluster of talents indicates a strength in overseeing the activities of others. These are essential for churches 350-plus. Should a youth pastor demonstrate one of these, it could clash with the senior pastor if he does not have one of these talents. Not useful talents for an associate pastor, unless he's an executive pastor.

> **Initiating/Developing.** The *church-planter* talent. It also is the *change-agent* talent and the *turnaround* talent. It needs a new project approximately every two years to stay in the same church.

> **Planning (Long-Range).** May or may not work well for a senior pastor, because the benefit of the talent will be determined by a person's other talents. This talent is vital for a large church as part of the senior executive team.

> **Managing.** Serves as a type of general manager, ensuring that the key players on the team are performing at their optimum capacities. It is essential for any church 350-plus that wants to grow. Can be a strength for the executive pastor.

Physical Coordination. A great talent for youth pastors.

Helping Talents—Any of this cluster of talents will color and shape the pastor's ministry to be more the shepherding style of caregiving. Favor churches less than three hundred. Youth pastors with any of these will demonstrate a more caregiving role, support for the marginalized and underdog.

Tutoring.

Being of Service.

Counseling.

Reassuring and Supporting.

Analyzing. Enjoys searching the depth of many issues. Can be too academic for the average church attendee. Not recommended for a youth pastor.

Calculating. Favors budgets and finances.

Problem Solving. Brings a host of benefits, including discernment for staff hiring, selection of lay leaders, in-depth sermon topic preparation, and settlement of disputes. It is valuable for resolving church conflicts. May not be best for a youth pastor.

Promoting. Adds much excitement and motivation to the pulpit, to fundraising, and to most any endeavor that seeks the participation or approval of others; favors evangelism outreach. Helpful also for youth pastors.

Researching. Brings a wealth of supplemental material for sermon preparation.

Technical Troubleshooting. Equips a pastor to do necessary repairs.

BIBLIOGRAPHY

Blackaby, Henry and Richard. *Spiritual Leadership*. Broadman and Holman Publishers, 2001.

Bolles, Richard. *What Color Is Your Parachute?* Berkley: Ten Speed Press, 2009.

Brennfleck, Kevin, and Kay Marie Brennfleck. *Live Your Calling*. San Francisco: Jossey-Bass, 2005.

Buckingham, Marcus and Curt Coffman. *First Break All the Rules*. New York: Simon & Schuster, 1999.

Buford, Bob. *Drucker and Me*. Brentwood: Worthy Publishing, 2014.

Cattell, Heather. *The 16PF Personality in-Depth*. Champaign: Institute for Personality and Ability Testing, Inc., 1989.

Collins, Jim. *Good to Great*. New York: Harper Collins Publishers, 2001.

Crabtree, J. Russell. *The Fly in the Ointment*. Church Publishing, 2008.

DePree, Max. *Leadership Is an Art*. New York: Dell Publishing, 1989.

Drucker, Peter. *Management*. New York: Harper & Row. 1974.

Drucker, Peter. *Managing for Results*. New York: Harper Collins Publishers, 1964.

Getz, Gene. *Elders and Leaders*. Chicago: Moody Publishers, 2003.

Gladwell, Malcolm. *Blink*. New York: Little, Brown and Company, 2005.

Guinness, Os. *The Call*. Nashville: Word Publishing, 1998.

Haldane, Bernard. *Career Satisfaction and Success*. New York: AMACON Publishers, 1974.

Hanson, Amy. *Baby Boomers and Beyond*. San Francisco: Jossey-Bass, 2010.

Hillman, George. *Ministry Greenhouse*. Herndon: The Alban Institute, 2008.

Hillman, George. *Preparing for Ministry*. Grand Rapids: Kregel Publications, 2008.

Hybels, Bill. *Courageous Leadership*. Grand Rapids: Zondervan, 2002.

Hyun, Jane. *Breaking the Bamboo Ceiling*. New York: Harper Collins Publishers, 2005.

Knopf, Gregory. *Demystifying Depression for Christians*. Troutdale, Oregon: In the Light Communications, 2011.

Kouzes, James, and Barry Posner. *Christian Reflections on The Leadership Challenge,* Third Edition. San Francisco: Jossey-Bass, 2004.

Kouzes, James, and Barry Posner. *The Leadership Challenge,* Third Edition. San Francisco: Jossey-Bass, 2002.

Lencioni, Patrick. *The Five Dysfunctions of a Team*. San Francisco: Jossey-Bass, 2002.

Lovejoy, Gary, and Gregory Knopf. *Light in the Darkness*. Indianapolis: Wesleyan Publishing, 2014.

Lucado, Max. *Cure for the Common Life*. Nashville: Thomas Nelson Publishers, 2005.

Miller, Linda, and Chad Hall. *Coaching for Christian Leaders*. St. Louis: Chalice Press, 2007.

Olson, David T. *Discovering Your Leadership Style*. InterVarsity Press, 2014.

Rainer, Thom. *Breakout Churches*. Grand Rapids: Zondervan, 2005.

Robbins, Alexandra, and Abby Wilner. *Quarterlife Crisis*. New York: Penguin Putnam, 2001.

Rusaw, Rick, and Eric Swanson. *The Externally Focused Church*. Loveland: Group Publishing, 2004.

Smith, Gordon. *Courage and Calling*. Downer's Grove: InterVarsity Press, 1999.

Smith, Terry. *Changing Course*. Saint Charles: Church Smart Resources, 2014.

Swanson, Eric, and Sam Williams. *To Transform a City*. Grand Rapids: Zondervan, 2010.

Taylor, Robert, and Lucile Morrison. *T-JTA Manual*. Thousand Oaks: Psychological Publications, 2007.

Tripp, Paul David. *Dangerous Calling*. Crossway Publishing, 2012.

Doctoral Dissertations Focusing on IDAK's Natural Talents

Harrell, David. *Hemispheric Dominance and Inherent Aptitudes*. Oxford Graduate School, Dayton, Tennessee, 1989.

Leighton, Arvid. *Development of the Manual for IDAK Career Match*. Rosemead School of Psychology, La Mirada, California, 1986.

McCarthy, David. *An Examination of the Relationship Between Student Vocational Talents and Freshman Satisfaction, Academic Achievement, and Retention at a Small Private College*. University of Georgia, Athens, Georgia, 1999.

ABOUT THE AUTHORS

Dr. Don Wiggins has served as superintendent of the C&MA North Central District since 2006. Don and Linda live in Waconia, Minnesota, and are the parents of five married children with sixteen grandchildren. All five kids are involved in C&MA ministry as pastors, pastor's wives, or international workers. Both Don and Linda graduated from Crown College, where they met. After they married, Don earned his MDiv at Trinity Evangelical Divinity School and later his DMin. He pastored churches in Fort Myers, Florida; Atlanta, Georgia; and Westmont, Illinois; and taught preaching and pastoral ministries at Toccoa Falls College and Crown College. Prior to coming to the North Central District, Don served in two capacities at the C&MA national office, including five years as vice president for Church Ministries, and he served four years as superintendent of the Great Lakes District.

Dr. John Bradley is founder and president of the IDAK Group in Portland, Oregon, and has specialized in aptitude assessment for more than forty-three years. He provides individual assessments and trains educators, organization executives, and counselor/consultants to provide these services for their respective organizations and consults to help campuses provide assessment for their students. His client organizations include Fortune 500 companies, family-owned businesses, and government agencies, as well as church denominations and mission agencies. Over six hundred professionals have used IDAK's assessment systems, assisting more than 30,000 individuals. John has served the Christian and Missionary Alliance from 1990 to the present.

John has earned a BA in Speech and Communication from the University of California at Davis, an MDiv from Western Seminary, and a Doctorate of Humane Letters from Faith Evangelical Seminary. His numerous radio and television appearances have included Focus on the Family, The 700 Club, and Moody's Midday Connection. His publications include *Follow Your Calling* (NavPress), *Switching Tracks* (Baker), *Discovering Your Natural Talents* with video (NavPress), and *Christian Career Planning* (Multnomah). He has led the development of the IDAK Career Match, the Talent Discovery Guide, and the MAX Profile Report.

IDAK ASSESSMENT INSTRUMENTS

The following IDAK aptitude assessment procedures and instruments are referred to in the text of this book. Information and samples can be obtained at *www.idakgroup.com*.

Autobiographical Interview
This interview assessment is the premier of all IDAK's procedures and instruments. It is available through Level III or Advanced Training.

Career Match
This assessment instrument is the premier career advancement instrument of IDAK's services. It matches an individual's interests, values, and natural talents to 90,000 career options. This was used in the first ten years of the Alliance training.

MAX Prime Report
This online assessment represents the same traits as the MAX Profile Report. It is used for first- and second-generation multicultural pastor candidates. Exercises are translated into Spanish, Hmong, Cambodian, Vietnamese, and South Korean. It is available through training and is the primary multicultural assessment used by the C&MA.

MAX Profile Report
This online assessment includes three online exercises: 16PF, TJTA, and the Talent Discovery Guide. It is available through training and is the primary report used by the C&MA.

Talent Discovery Guide
This assessment instrument is available online at *www.ida-kgroup.com/tdg* and is also part of the MAX Profile Report.

Validation Interview
This interview assessment is an abbreviated version of the Autobiographical Interview. It is the primary interview process used by the Alliance. It is available through training and normally is combined with MAX Report training.

ENDNOTES

[1] Peter Drucker, "Managing Oneself," *Harvard Business Review*, January 2005, 100-101; reprinted from *Management Challenges for the Twenty-First Century* (New York: Harper Collins), 1999.

[2] Bill Hybels, *Courageous Leadership* (Grand Rapids: Zondervan), 2002.

[3] H.B. London, *Pastor's Weekly Briefing*.

[4] January 2011, online.

[5] "How Are We Doing?" *Auburn Studies,* December 2007, 5. We know of no long-term studies that reliably measure the dropout rate in ministry. A few other thoughtful sources: "Do Seminary Grads Burn Out Quickly?" *Transformed,* Western Seminary online publication, April 18, 2012, www.westernseminary.edu; "How Many Quit? Estimating the Clergy Attrition Rate," Into Action, www.into-action.net/research/many-quit-estimating-clergy-attrition-rate; Chris Maxwell, "Runaway Shepherds?" *Ministry Today,* www.ministrytodaymag.com.

[6] K. A. Ericsson, R. Th. Krampe, and C. Tesch-Römer, "The role of deliberate practice in the acquisition of expert performance," *Psychological Review*, 1993, 100(3), 363-406.

[7] Brooke N. Macnamara, David Z. Hambrick, and Frederick L. Oswald, "Deliberate Practice and Performance in Music, Games, Sports, Education, and Professions: A Meta-Analysis," *Psychological Science*, August 2014, vol. 25, no. 8.

[8] Jessica Dickler, "Stressful Jobs that Pay Badly," www.money.cnn.com/galleries/2009/pf/0910/gallery.stressful_jobs/10.html.

THE**ALLIANCE**

The Alliance in the United States comprises more than 2,000 churches, mobilized to fulfill the Great Commission (Matthew 28:18–20) by living out the fullness of Jesus Christ in personal experience and building His Church worldwide. Seven hundred U.S.-based Alliance workers serve in 70 countries.